the laboratory detectives

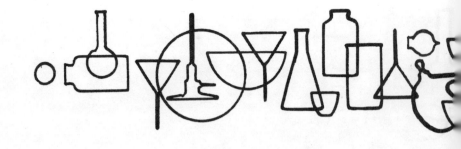

the laboratory detectives

HOW SCIENCE TRAPS THE CRIMINAL

Norman Lucas

Taplinger Publishing Company | New York

First published in the United States in 1972 by
TAPLINGER PUBLISHING CO., INC.
New York, New York

Library of Congress Catalog Card Number: 74-185483

ISBN 0-8008-4515-3

For Betty Harley

With grateful thanks for her invaluable assistance
in the compilation of this book

Contents

Foreword

The need to develop and co-ordinate scientific methods as an aid to criminal investigation was realized at the beginning of the twentieth century when a forensic science laboratory was established at Lyons, France and a school for the training of police scientific experts was founded at Lausanne.

At about the same time, similar laboratories were set up in Vienna and Brussels.

In Britain, police and forensic science laboratories were not established for some years, and the first was set up by a local force at Nottingham by the then Chief Constable, Captain Athelstan Popkess. He founded the Nottingham Laboratory in 1932. It still exists and serves police forces in the East Midlands area.

Two years later, Lord Trenchard established Scotland Yard's Forensic Laboratory and the Home Office gradually organized regional laboratories at Birmingham, Llanishen, Preston, Harrogate, Newcastle upon Tyne and Bristol.

The value of forensic science in the day and night battle with the criminal can never be over-estimated. Although it is only during the past thirty-five years that its full importance has been recognized in Britain, it has a significant historical background.

A crude technique of forensic science was employed as far back as 1786, when a girl living in Kircudbrightshire, Scotland, was found by her parents lying murdered in their cottage. A man strongly suspected of the killing was arrested, but he produced what appeared to be a cast-iron alibi. A close examination of the scene of the crime revealed footprints. For the first time in British criminal history, plaster casts were taken of the prints. The pattern of the hobnails was identical with that produced by the man's boots.

9

Socks he had worn were found to be impregnated with the dead woman's blood, and mud and sand particles in the wool had, it was established after tests, come from around the cottage. The man was tried at Dumfries in the spring of 1787 and convicted mainly on this evidence.

It was not until the early twentieth century, however, that the bio-chemical analysis of blood could be directly related to the detection of crime. In 1902 evidence based upon tests perfected by the French biochemist Bordet was accepted in English courts. Nevertheless 'expert' forensic science witnesses were always strongly attacked during the next quarter of a century when they appeared in court. Lawyers made every attempt possible to discredit them and the newly developed branch of scientific detection.

Today, the forensic experts frequently provide the vital supporting evidence that detectives need to convict those guilty of heinous killings. Throughout the laboratories, chemical and biological sections are overburdened with work.

In general, the chemists deal with breaking offences and road accidents; analysis of body fluids for alcohol; toxicological analysis; addictive drugs and narcotic identifications; a variety of miscellaneous matters such as the restoration of erased identification marks on stolen property (often the engine and chassis numbers on stolen cars); and the investigation of arson, counterfeiting and forgery.

Biologists deal mainly with offences against people – murders, woundings (by shooting, poisoning or stabbing), rape or any other sexual assault and ordinary assault.

In this age when the number of offences daily continues to spiral upwards, the laboratory detectives find that the hours evaporate as swiftly as the pure spirit in their test tubes.

1

The strange lodger

Blood and bullets, leaves and lipstick, dust and dirt, human and animal hairs, household fluff, cloth fibres, tyre tracks – all these, in the past fifty years, have helped to prove criminals guilty of crimes. But not long after the turn of the century, when inks and pen-nibs were almost as individual as handwriting, and ballpoint was a word yet to be invented, one of the first murderers trapped in the web of forensic science was convicted largely on the evidence of a bottle of ink. Apart from many bizarre features which, in retrospect, make the crime seem more like fiction than fact, it was a case of some significance because it was among the first in which scientific evidence was admitted in a court of law in Britain.

The story began in the summer of 1906 when a jobbing gardener called Richard Brinkley took lodgings with a seventy-six-year-old German widow, Mrs Johanna Maria Blume, at 4 Maxwell Road, Fulham, London SW6. From the beginning, Brinkley seems to have been a man of mystery. He was said to be married and the father of four children, but either his wife had left him or he had deserted his family, because none of them was named and all kept discreetly anonymous during the period of Brinkley's later notoriety. His age, too, was uncertain, but he was thought to be in his fifties. Even his appearance was not all it seemed. Mrs Blume's lodger was a handsome, dashing fellow, with a fine head of black hair and a splendid black moustache which curled up at the ends. The same man, a year later, deprived of his wig, black dye, wax and curling tongs, was a pathetic near-bald old chap with a drooping, grey walrus moustache.

The Richard Brinkley of 1906 was well liked by old Mrs Blume and she was delighted when, on 17 December that year, he told her that he was arranging a picnic outing to take place

11

in the spring. He promised 'great jollifications' and the old lady happily put her signature to a folded sheet of foolscap which purported to be a list of persons willing to participate in this 'beanfeast'.

On the same day Brinkley visited a friend, Reginald Clifford Parker, a middle-aged accountant's clerk who lodged at Churchill Road, South Croydon, Surrey, and invited him to join the same outing. Parker signed a sheet of paper on which he could see several other names, using for the purpose his own fountain-pen filled with a sepia-coloured ink called Tickit, apparently obtainable by very few people except chartered accountants.

The two men went for a walk together and while they were out Brinkley asked Parker if he would sign a second copy of the outing list. Parker demurred, saying that he did not see any necessity for two lists, and anyway he had left his fountain-pen at home. Brinkley, however, insisted. He took Parker into an off-licence where (without buying anything!) he borrowed pen and ink and handed his friend a folded sheet of paper which Parker signed, innocently supposing this to be Brinkley's second outing list.

Two days later, on 19 December 1906, old Mrs Blume died suddenly while she was alone in the house.

As she had apparently been in good health a post-mortem examination was performed. There was no sign of disease, but there were some small haemorrhages in the brain which were thought to be apoplectic in nature. An inquest was held by Mr S. Ingleby Oddie, then Deputy Coroner for West London, and the jury returned a verdict of natural death from cerebral haemorrhage. Mr Oddie, recalling this case many years later, confessed that he had never been quite happy about the cause of death because of the absence of the customary very large haemorrhages in the brain, but at the time he had no reason to be suspicious.

He was not to know that shortly after the inquest Richard Brinkley would produce an apparently valid will, signed by Mrs Blume and witnessed by Reginald Parker and a man called Henry Heard, in which Brinkley was appointed executor and sole legatee. The old lady had left him her house, furniture, stocks and cash to a total value of just under £800 – a

12

considerable sum in the days when a domestic servant was paid about £15 a year and thirty shillings a week was a princely wage for a working man.

Brinkley promptly moved into the house in Maxwell Road, and while waiting to get his hands on the old lady's money sold some of the furniture and pawned anything of value. His new status as a member of the 'moneyed classes' was, however, short-lived. He received notice that Mrs Blume's will was, not surprisingly, to be contested by her daughter Caroline, a middle-aged woman who ran a lodging-house in another part of London.

This raised considerable problems for Brinkley, who knew quite well that the will was a fraud from beginning to end. He had drafted the document himself and obtained the necessary signatures from Mrs Blume and at least one of the witnesses by duping them into believing that they were signing an agreement to take part in the much-vaunted spring outing.

But, nothing if not resourceful, Brinkley countered Miss Blume's move by proposing marriage to her – although they had met only once, at her mother's funeral. His faith in his persuasive charms was not justified. She turned him down, explaining in a later interview with a *Croydon Advertiser* reporter: 'Within a month of the funeral he asked me to marry him, saying it had been my mother's wish and that the property could then be enjoyed together. He was a stranger to me and I refused.'

Although a poorly educated man, Richard Brinkley was no fool, and he knew that the will, if contested, would have to be legally proved by the two witnesses swearing on oath that Mrs Blume had signed the will in their presence and that they had both put their signatures to the same document on the same occasion.

Brinkley decided that Reginald Parker must be killed before he could give the game away. There is no evidence as to whether or not he planned to dispose of the second witness, Henry Heard, after dealing with Parker. In fact there is so little information about this man Heard – apart from his address which was given as Hollydale Road, Peckham, London SE15 – that one wonders if he ever existed. It seems not improbable that Brinkley himself was the mysterious 'Henry Heard'.

This was only one of the many mysteries in the whole baffling affair. Another was the odd behaviour of Parker, who learned that Mrs Blume's will was to be contested and began to wonder about the papers he had signed at Brinkley's request. Evidence he gave later showed that for some months he went in fear of his life. He was sure that Brinkley planned to murder him, knew that the weapon would be poison, yet did nothing about it apart from a careful avoidance of any food or drink offered by Brinkley. It apparently did not occur to him to communicate his suspicions to the police, but he did mention his fears to friends, saying that if anything happened to him while he was with Brinkley they would know what to do. Yet he continued to see Brinkley, accepting invitations to go to the house at Fulham and raising no objections when Brinkley wanted to visit him at Croydon.

One evening Reg Parker went to Maxwell Road at Brinkley's request and found his host waiting for him with a bottle of whisky and two glasses – a circumstance which immediately made him suspicious because Brinkley, as a staunch member of the Sons of Temperance, had never been known to touch a drop of alcohol. As soon as Brinkley had poured the drinks he asked Parker to go to the kitchen for some water, no doubt, as Parker suspected, to give him the opportunity to slip something lethal into his friend's glass. Parker made an excuse to refuse the drink.

Brinkley then started to visit Parker at Croydon almost every evening, round about tea-time, and usually asked for a glass of water. Parker always obliged, leaving Brinkley alone in the room. But, apart from going without most of his tea-time meal on several occasions, poor Parker did nothing about what was rapidly becoming an uncomfortable situation.

This went on throughout the early spring of 1907 until the night of 20 April, when Brinkley went to Croydon on the pretext of buying a bulldog that Parker wanted to sell. The early part of the evening passed happily enough. When Brinkley arrived at Churchill Road he found his friend enjoying a glass of beer with his landlord, a middle-aged gardener called Richard Beck, and the three men were later joined by Beck's wife, Annie Elizabeth.

As soon as the Becks left Parker's room Brinkley produced

14

a bottle of oatmeal stout, which he said had been strongly recommended to him by a doctor. He poured some into a glass and, temporarily deserting his principles of abstinence, took a hearty swig. Parker drank some from the same glass, but declined any more after Brinkley had sent him from the room to fetch the usual glass of water.

The two men then took the dog for a walk and there was some discussion about how much Brinkley should pay for it and how best the animal, a rather ferocious beast, could be taken to Fulham. They parted in the street soon after 11.30 pm.

In the meantime the Becks, who had been out for part of the evening, had returned home. Mr Beck, seeing the opened bottle of stout in their lodger's room, invited his wife and elder daughter, Daisy, aged twenty-one, to join him in sampling the brew. Richard Beck drank half a glassful and so did his wife. Daisy took one sip, said it tasted bitter and spat it out.

Within a few seconds the Becks' younger daughter, nineteen-year-old Hilda, who had gone to bed, heard terrible noises coming from Parker's room. She rushed in to find both her parents and her sister lying unconscious on the floor, foaming at the mouth. Dr William Dempster, who lived nearby, was called, but by the time he arrived both Mr and Mrs Beck were dying in convulsions. Daisy was rushed to Croydon General Hospital, where she recovered within a few days.

Dr Dempster sniffed at the by now empty stout bottle – and smelt the unmistakable bitter-almond aroma of prussic acid. The police were called and poor Parker, who had been congratulating himself on having once again outwitted the murderous Brinkley, arrived home to find that he had escaped death at the cost of two other lives.

At this point, somewhat belatedly, he told the police the whole story of Mrs Blume's will, the papers he had signed, and his fear that Brinkley was trying to put him out of the way to stop him testifying. The following day Richard Brinkley was seen at Fulham and told he was to be charged with the murders of Richard and Annie Beck and with the attempted murders of Daisy Beck and Reginald Parker. 'This is very awkward, isn't it?' he said. 'I have not seen Parker for three weeks. Does he say I done it? He's a dirty bloody tyke and spiteful. I've got a good character and I'm a teetotaller. If anyone says I bought beer they've got to prove it.'

As beer had not till then been mentioned, this was an unfortunate remark. In any event it was simple enough to prove that Brinkley had bought the stout. A lad employed at an off-licence in Brighton Road, South Croydon, remembered him well as a man who had gone into the shop early in the evening of 20 April and asked for a bottle of this particular brand of oatmeal stout. The price of the stout was $2\frac{1}{2}$d, but an extra 2d was required as deposit on the bottle. Brinkley objected to this charge as excessive and offered $1\frac{1}{2}$d. He left the shop in a huff when this offer was refused, but returned within a few minutes and paid the full price, taking the bottle after it had been stamped with the name and address of the shop.

Further evidence of Brinkley's presence in Croydon was given by a railway inspector, who knew the man well by sight and said that on the evening in question he had bought a rail ticket from Fulham to Croydon.

How did Brinkley get the prussic acid?

A doctor's dispenser, William Vale, who lived at Manor Road, South Norwood, volunteered the information that Brinkley, an acquaintance, had on two occasions asked for something to poison a dog. Vale had obligingly supplied him with prussic acid.

On 4 May 1907, the body of old Mrs Blume was exhumed and examined by Sir Thomas Stevenson, a famous medico-legal expert of his day, but all tests for poison proved negative. Mr Ingleby Oddie afterwards admitted to being rather anxious about the results of this exhumation, fearing that he might have blundered in allowing the inquest jury to return a verdict of natural death, although on the evidence he could have taken no other course. As prussic acid is a very volatile poison and the old lady had been buried for more than four months, Mr Oddie was not surprised at the negative results of the analysis, but he believed very strongly that she had been murdered by Brinkley.

Whether or not Brinkley did kill Mrs Blume – after that lapse of time there was no hope of proving it one way or the other – the old lady's will was of paramount importance when the double murder and attempted murder trial took place before Mr Justice Bigham at Guildford Assizes in July 1907. If the will had proved to be genuine Brinkley would have had no reason to attempt to kill Reginald Parker and Parker himself would have been shown as a liar whose evidence, as the main witness for the prosecution, would necessarily have been highly suspect.

Mr R. D. Muir, prosecuting, produced his trump card in the person of Mr Charles Mitchell, a Fellow of the Institute of Chemistry. Mr Mitchell told the court that the will and signatures had been subjected to careful chemical analysis. He found that three different inks had been used – one for the body of the will and the signature of Henry Heard, a second for Mrs Blume's signature, and a third for the signature of Reginald Parker. Analysis of the ink at the off-licence at which Parker said he had signed the second copy of the outing list showed it to be the same as the ink of his signature on the will. His name on the genuine outing list had been signed with his fountain-pen filled with Tickit ink.

Brinkley, who was defended by Mr Walter Frampton, tried to confuse the issue by saying that Mrs Blume kept three bottles of different inks in her house, but a search of the property had already shown there to be only one bottle, the contents of which matched the old lady's signature. No trace had been found of the ink used for the main body of the will and the signature of Henry Heard – and this apparently phantom figure was conspicuous by his absence from the trial. He was mentioned by neither prosecution nor defence, although Mr Justice Bigham, in his summing-up, pointed out that he was the one person, apart from Parker, who could have testified to the signing of the will.

The jury took fifty-five minutes to find Brinkley guilty on all charges. He was sentenced to death and – protesting his innocence to the end – was hanged at Wandsworth jail on 10 August 1907.

2

Accident! – or murder?

It was ten o'clock on the night of Thursday, 2 March 1967. Robin Franklin, a fireman, of Knights Way, Emmer Green, Berkshire, was driving with a friend, Colin Pinfield, along a narrow, winding lane between Hook End and Peppard, near Henley-on-Thames, Oxfordshire. As the road passed through lonely Rumerhedge Wood the headlights of their car illuminated a driverless blue Cortina. The sidelights of the Ford were on and the lid of the boot open. It was parked on a bend. Robin Franklin had some difficulty in edging past the car. He had hardly negotiated the bend when the two men noticed a red Mini, off the road. A woman was lying beside it and the shadowy figure of a man was crouched over her. They both noticed another man in the passenger seat of the Mini.

The whole scene was a frightening tableau. Franklin jumped out of his car and asked if he could help. The man looking at the woman straightened up. 'No,' he replied, adding that he was going back to his own car to get some towels. He walked in the direction of the Cortina. Mr Franklin heard the sounds of the boot being closed, a door slamming, and then a roar as the car was driven away. The mysterious stranger disappeared into the night, leaving Franklin and Pinfield to call an ambulance for the obviously badly injured woman.

At Battle Hospital, Reading, it was discovered that the woman had terrible head injuries. She died at twenty minutes after midnight.

The man who had been sitting in the passenger seat of the red Mini had only a small abrasion to his left knee.

It was established that he was Raymond Sidney Cook, a thirty-two-year-old draughtsman, and that the dead woman was his wife, June Serena, aged forty-one, a schoolteacher.

The couple's home was at Farley View, Spencers Wood, Reading. That fateful evening they had dined together – on scampi, steak and a bottle of Beaujolais – at the riverside George Hotel in Pangbourne. Then, according to Cook, his wife had started to drive them home. He told doctors at the hospital that he could only remember seeing headlights coming towards them and a tree 'looming up'. He thought his wife had been dazzled by the glare and had driven off the road, hitting the tree.

Just another tragic road accident, a terrible sequel to a happy outing or . . . It was a young constable appropriately named Sherlock who first suspected that all might not be quite as it seemed. PC Stephen Sherlock, twenty-six-year-old village bobby stationed at Nettlebed, near Henley, was called to the scene of the crash and later saw Mrs Cook's body in hospital. He was told that her injuries could have been caused by her being flung through the windscreen and hitting her head on a tree – but Sherlock had already noticed that the windscreen was intact and the Mini only very slightly damaged.

He was so puzzled that he returned to the scene of the crash in the early hours of the morning and there, by the light of his flashlamp, found blood on the road more than fifty yards from the Mini. Another officer examined the car and established that it was roadworthy and had been travelling at not more than ten miles an hour when it hit the tree.

Dr Derek Ford Barrowcliff, Home Office pathologist, told detectives that Mrs Cook, who had died from a compound fracture of the skull, had received at least seven separate injuries to her scalp. There was no glass or gravel in the wounds and he did not believe that the injuries could have been caused by her being in the car when it collided with a tree. They could have been inflicted by a car jack.

Accident? Detective Chief Inspector Wooldridge, chief of Reading CID, thought it was beginning to look more like murder, and within a few days of the woman's death two Scotland Yard men – Detective Superintendent (now Deputy Assistant Commissioner) Ian Forbes and Detective Sergeant Peter Hill – arrived in Reading to take charge of inquiries.

The funeral, arranged for 10 March, was stopped on their instructions, and an appeal was made for the driver of the blue Cortina seen parked near the scene of the crash to come forward.

Raymond Cook stuck to his story of an accident, but the police did not believe him and he was arrested outside Reading Coroner's Court a few minutes after the inquest had been opened and adjourned on 17 March. Told that he would be charged with the murder of his wife, Cook said, 'I understand'.

After nation-wide inquiries the Cortina, registration number 7711 FM, was found to belong to Eric Jones, a forty-six-year-old plant manager, of Chester Road, Wrexham, Denbighshire, more than a hundred miles away. He was seen by Detective Sergeant Charles Matthews, of Wrexham, who knew Jones to be an undischarged bankrupt and a suspected abortionist – but that did not make him a murderer and Jones was emphatic that he had not been near Reading on 2 March. Matthews was suspicious, however, particularly when Jones confidently assured him, 'You'll find nothing here.'

It was, in fact, what Matthews did *not* find at Jones's home that clinched it. The jack was missing from his blue Cortina. It seemed probable, if it was the jack that had been used to bludgeon Mrs Cook to death, that it would have been disposed of somewhere near Jones's home. A search of lakes and ponds in the area yielded results. Frogmen discovered the missing jack in a yachting pool called Gresford Flash, not far from Wrexham.

In Reading further evidence was beginning to mount against Jones. A painter called Angus McDonald, of Lower Henley Road, Caversham, went to the police and told them that he had seen the blue Cortina in the Reading area on the night of 2 March, and had followed it for about a mile. It was being driven by a man who was a stranger to him, but he had recognized the passenger as a girl called Valerie ('Kim') Newell, who lived next door to his mother in Sidmouth Street, Reading.

The pieces were beginning to fit . . . because by this time the police had ample evidence that Raymond Cook and Valerie Newell, an attractive, twenty-three-year-old blonde, had not only worked together for a short period, but had been lovers for six months – and that Eric Jones was a former lover of

20

the girl. Cook and Kim had made no secret of their affair, or of the fact that Cook's wife, June, was greatly in the way. Just before Christmas 1966 they visited a Jamaican friend, Mr Cleland Thompson, of Southcote, Reading, and Kim told him she would kill Mrs Cook if she thought she could get away with it. She added, 'If you know anyone who could do the job it would pay them to do it.'

At about the same period there was a conversation between Eric Jones and Kim in front of Mrs Susan Heslop, who at that time was living at the same address as Miss Newell. Jones, Mrs Heslop and Kim drove to an old airfield which was described by Kim as a 'suitably quiet place'. There was talk between Jones and Kim of getting Mrs Cook drunk while she was out with her car in the hope that she would 'finish up in the river'. Mrs Heslop got the impression that they might be going to drown Mrs Cook.

After Raymond Cook had been arrested Kim visited her sister, Mrs Janet Adams, of Lower Way, Thatcham, Berkshire, and – perhaps because she was by then frightened and felt that she had to unburden her guilt to someone – confessed that the 'accident' was in fact a prearranged murder planned by Cook, Jones and herself and actually carried out by Jones.

But following this visit, Kim Newell had second thoughts about her confession. By the time this incident occurred, Reading was full of national newspaper men. Among them were two of Fleet Street's finest reporters, Eddie Laxton of the *Daily Mirror* and Kenneth Parrish of the *London Evening News*.

I met Eddie and Ken in a Reading club. They were both convinced that Kim Newell was one of the architects of the crime, if not in fact the number-one planner. I decided that I would visit the blonde Kim. At first she was reluctant to talk, but eventually, with a sweet smile that did not match the machinations of her mind, she brazenly announced that the finger of suspicion was unjustifiably being pointed at her. 'I was not having an affair with Ray Cook,' she said. 'I admit that we were friends but I was no more friendly with him that I was with his wife.'

But Kim Newell's denials came too late. After days of agonized indecision, Mrs Adams had walked into Reading police station and told the whole story.

21

On 18 April 1967, just a month after Raymond Cook's arrest, Eric Jones and Kim Newell were also charged with the murder of June Cook, and the whole story of the association of these characters – reading more like something from the sleazier type of detective fiction than from the pages of real life – was slowly unfolded.

Valerie Dorothy Newell was the younger daughter of Frank Newell, an army staff sergeant from London who settled in Wales after the war. She and her sister Janet grew up on a farm estate at Rhos-y-Madoc, near Ruabon, Denbighshire, leading rather narrow, sheltered lives in which church activities – both sang in the choir – played the biggest part. Kim, as Valerie became known, was a remarkably pretty child. By the time she was fifteen she was a beautiful very mature young woman, full-breasted, with long, slim legs and shining blonde hair. She was not lacking in personality either and her gay, fun-loving nature helped to attract the lads of the village. But her first lover was no lad. He was Eric Jones, an ex-Marine and tree-felling expert who augmented his income by abortions at fifty pounds a time and who was to feature so prominently during her love triangle with Cook. Before her seventeenth birthday Kim was pregnant by Jones, but he soon disposed of the unborn child, leaving the girl free to pursue her life of gaiety.

When she was eighteen she left home to become a children's nurse in Oxford, quickly losing not only her Welsh accent but any inhibitions remaining from her strict Welsh upbringing. During associations with wealthy undergraduates at the university she developed a taste for luxury – a taste which was soon indulged by rich business men who easily succumbed to her sexy charms. A race-horse breeder, a well-known bookmaker and a playboy with a Rolls-Royce were among her patrons. She became pregnant four more times and on each occasion Eric Jones performed abortions.

From Oxford she moved to Reading, where the pattern of sexual conquests was soon repeated. At one stage she became engaged to the son of an ex-London policeman, but there was apparently never a time when she had less than two lovers and the engagement was broken off.

In 1966 Kim gave up being a children's nanny to take a

22

nursing job at Borocourt Mental Hospital near Reading. It was here that she met Raymond Cook. This slightly balding man over six feet four inches tall, who was described at the murder trial as 'a sort of silent lumpkin', was not on the face of it a likely candidate for Valerie Newell's attentions, but he was a free spender and she might at first have believed him to be wealthy.

In fact he had little money of his own. He had been trained as a draughtsman and for some years worked at the Handley Page aircraft factory at Woodley, near Reading. While there he met and married a woman nine years his senior whose first marriage to an army officer had ended in divorce. When Handley Page closed their Woodley factory in 1963 Cook became redundant and his wife, June, a teacher of mentally retarded children, persuaded him to embark on a new career of mental nursing. Although the couple had two children, Cook was able to enrol as a low-paid student nurse because their house had been a gift from his wife's parents and June had other assets in the form of property, insurance stocks and cash in the bank – she was worth about £11,000.

Within a few weeks of their first meeting Cook and Kim had become lovers. He was quite besotted with her. He cashed a £700 insurance policy to give her the things she coveted – clothes, expensive perfumes, meals and drinks at the best hotels. It was nothing for him to spend £30 a week on entertainment for her and within four months the £700 had gone.

He failed his nursing examinations, for which he had worked for three years, and resigned from the hospital. Kim, too, lost her job – and once again became pregnant. Mrs Cook found out about their association and made a new will under the terms of which all her property was to be held in trust for the two children and there would be nothing for her husband.

The lovers were by now living together, but cash was running short. Kim made another trip to Wales to see Eric Jones, but this time she had Cook with her – and she wasn't asking for an abortion. The three of them met in a Chinese restaurant just before Christmas 1966, and it was agreed between them that Jones would 'get rid of' Mrs Cook. He was

23

given £100 in notes and promised £1,000 when the job was done.

Several alternative plots were discussed, but it was eventually decided that a fake car accident would be the best method because Mrs Cook held an insurance policy which paid £1,000 bonus for death by accident. But first they had to make sure that the money would go to Cook after his wife's death – so he returned to June and told her that his affair with Newell had ended. His wife was happy to believe him and made another will under which her husband was once more the chief beneficiary.

To the wretched doomed woman that evening of 2 March 1967 seemed an occasion for celebration because she thought that her husband was getting over his infatuation and that he and she would soon be happy together again. She arranged for a baby-sitting agency to supply a girl to look after the children and had a special hair-do so that she would look her best for this 'forgive and forget' outing.

Three versions of the plot to dispose of Mrs Cook and three versions of events on the night of her death were heard when Cook, Jones and Valerie Newell stood in the dock before Mr Justice Stable and a jury of ten men and two women at Oxfordshire Assizes in June 1967. Jones and Cook were jointly charged with her murder. Miss Newell, originally also accused of murder, was charged with being an accessory before the fact 'in that she counselled, procured and hired' the two men to commit the murder.

All three at first pleaded not guilty, but Eric Jones later changed his plea to guilty, was sentenced to life imprisonment and then called as a witness for the prosecution. Jones told the court that when he met Kim and Cook in December 1966 he asked the girl if she was wanting another abortion and she replied: 'No, something bigger.' She then said she wanted him to smash a Mini car, because she and her lover intended to get rid of Mrs Cook. Several plans were made and on one occasion Kim showed Jones a narrow hump-back bridge and asked him if he could run Mrs Cook off the road into the river at that spot. He replied that the river was not deep enough.

Describing events on 2 March, Jones said that he picked up

24

Miss Newell in Reading. She showed him the direction from which the Mini would come and pointed out the tree into which he was to run the car. 'I asked her how she expected a Mini to run into a tree and kill Mrs Cook. She was evasive and said all I had to worry about was to run the Mini into the tree and help Cook make it look like an accident. Then I was to hit him on the chin as though he had been knocked out. I kept finding excuses and she got mad. I said I would get into trouble with my wife if I did not get back by midnight and she replied that I would get in a bloody sight more trouble if I left. She reminded me I could get eight years for abortion and said she had policemen in Reading who used to go up to her flat at night for coffee and they would expose me.'

After looking at the tree, continued Jones, he drove Miss Newell back to Reading and then returned to the appointed place. When the red Mini came along Cook got out and told him to 'get on with it'. They both went up to the Mini and Cook asked Mrs Cook if she would mind giving him, Jones, a lift into town as his car, the Cortina, had a flat tyre.

Mr Brian Gibbens QC, leading for the Crown asked Jones: 'Is it right you struck Mrs Cook with an implement?' The witness replied: 'Yes.'

'Did Mr Cook take any part in the actual violence on Mrs Cook?' asked the judge. 'None, sir,' replied Jones. 'He handed me the jack. I snatched it out of his hand and struck Mrs Cook.'

Afterwards, he said, he ran the car into the tree while Cook and Mrs Cook were both in the vehicle. He stood on the sill of the driving door, putting one foot on the throttle and one hand on the steering wheel while Cook started the car and put it in gear. Later when Mrs Cook was lying on the ground, he hit her again with the jack.

Cross-examined by Mr Douglas Draycott QC, for Cook, Jones agreed that nothing was said in Cook's presence about killing Mrs Cook when there was talk of getting rid of her. Miss Newell had told him that Cook would not have the guts to do anything about it.

Mr Draycott: 'You are telling the jury that Miss Newell forced you?' – 'In a way, yes.'

25

'The reason you are saying this is that it will make your position seem better ' – ' No, sir.'

'You say you were not intending to kill and that by sheer bad luck at the psychological moment someone put a jack in your hand?' – 'Yes.'

In reply to a question from Mr William Howard QC, for Valerie Newell, Jones agreed that he dated Miss Newell, whom he first met in a secondary school playground in 1959 when he was thirty-seven.

Mr Howard: 'Was it not obvious she was a schoolchild?' – 'No.'

'How old did you think she was?' – 'About sixteen or seventeen.'

'Having seduced her you then introduced her to abortion?' – 'Not as you put it.'

'Did she become with child and did you abort her?' – 'I did.'

Before giving his version of the events of 2 March, Raymond Cook told the court that his relationship with his wife had deteriorated before he met Valerie Newell, with whom he lived for seven weeks towards the end of 1966. On 4 November that year he visited his wife and she persuaded him to stay. If he had not done so she would have ensured that he would not have any money. She told him she was fed up with living and he came to the conclusion that she might commit suicide.

He met Eric Jones when he went with Miss Newell to see her parents at Wrexham in December 1966. 'I had heard he was an abortionist and was involved in any racket going,' said Cook. 'At our first meeting I talked about divorce and medical drugs and how Jones could acquire them. He talked about his abortions and how much money he had made on them.' Cook added that he got the impression that Jones would like to help him and Miss Newell to get married and was given to understand that Jones might be able to arrange something ' on the lines of a divorce '. He gave Jones £100 because he thought the man was going to help them.

Replying to questions by Mr Gibbens, Cook agreed that he had arranged for his wife ' to be removed and kept away ' so that a divorce could be concocted against her. He knew that

26

absence of three years was needed as grounds of desertion but it was not his plan that his wife should be removed for three years.

Mr Gibbens: 'Was it your idea that concocted photographs would show her in a position of adultery?' – 'Possibly.'

'Do you accept that if your wife was not willing to be photographed in an act of adultery she would have to be forced?' – 'Yes.'

'That would be rape, wouldn't it?' – 'I had not envisaged photographs of the type suggested.'

Asked why he could not continue living with Miss Newell without the removal of his wife, Cook replied: 'My wife's health was not good.'

'Was it going to improve her health to have her abducted and kept in enforced imprisonment against her will and without her children?' – 'No.' Cook added that it had been intended that his wife was to sustain concussion in the car smash, to wander off and then be picked up by Jones.

'What about explanations to your wife's parents?' – 'I was not on speaking terms with them.'

Mr Justice Stable: 'Are you asking the jury to believe that your wife's mother and father, who lived next door, would not ask what had happened?' – 'We were not talking.'

Turning to the night of 2 March 1967, Cook said he phoned Jones and told him that he had found a suitable place 'to pick up the parcel', as he had been told that when he telephoned he must refer to Mrs Cook as 'the parcel'. When they met at the appointed place Jones got into the back of the Mini. 'I thought he was going to drug my wife with chloroform,' continued Cook. 'The door shut and I walked to the front of Jones's car. Jones seemed to stagger out of the Mini. He was swearing and I could see he was punching. I went to hit Jones, but he moved. He was still punching away. He must have realized I was coming because he turned and hit me in the stomach and I was winded. Jones made for the boot of his car and grabbed something from it. As he turned I could see that it was a jack. He seemed to have gone berserk. He rushed back to the Mini, grabbed my wife's hair and then started hitting her, two or three blows in as many seconds . . .' Cook's voice faltered and the judge adjourned the proceedings for a few minutes. Cook then went on to say that Jones ordered him to get into the Mini.

'I was terrified. I do not remember starting the car. Jones was pressing the accelerator and the Mini went forward and collided with a tree. . . . I hit my head on some part of the car and found myself on the road and I lost consciousness. When I came round I got back in. My wife wasn't in the car but I could hear the sound of her breathing. Jones had the jack in his hand . . . then he went away and the lights of another car appeared.'

Under cross-examination Cook agreed that he did not make any serious attempt to stop Jones, adding 'I have never used violence against anybody. I have never been in a fight with anyone.'

Mr Gibbens held up the jack and asked: 'Here was a man slaughtering your wife – and because you never used violence to any man before you didn't think of trying to save your wife?' Cook did not reply and Mr Gibbens then asked him: 'Do I take it you made no effort to defend your wife?'

'I made a pathetic attempt,' replied Cook. 'You made no attempt whatsoever.' – 'I made very little.' Replying to Mr Howard, Cook said he was very frightened of Jones after having seen what he had done that night. He moved his children to London so that Jones would not know their whereabouts and had also told Miss Newell to leave her flat in Reading.

On the ninth day of the trial Valerie Newell, wearing a beige maternity smock, went into the witness-box. She sat on a pile of red cushions as she gave evidence for two days and answered questions from the three counsels and the judge.

She said that in November 1966 she telephoned Jones to ask him to perform an abortion as she did not want the child. Jones asked her why she did not marry Cook and she explained that he was already married. There was some conversation about 'losing' wives in which Jones said that he had drugged wives and lost them for six months so that their husbands could file for divorce. He took the wives to Liverpool where 'his boys looked after them'. 'Did you believe him?' asked Mr Howard, and Miss Newell replied: 'No, I

28

thought he was being terribly boastful and bragging, his normal self.'

Cook, however, seemed fascinated by Jones's stories of abortions and losing wives when the two men met at a later date. At the time Cook told her that Jones was going to kidnap Mrs Cook she asked Jones what he intended to do and Jones said he was expecting £1,000 for the kidnapping. Miss Newell continued: 'I said to him, "You are not going to harm her in any way, are you?" and he laughed and said something to the effect that killing was not his business. I said if no harm came to Mrs Cook I would ask Ray [Mr Cook] to give him a further £500.'

On the evening of 2 March she and Cook had an argument because Cook asked her to meet Jones and take him to a place he had chosen for the kidnapping of Mrs Cook. 'He produced a map and showed me where I was to go, but I said I did not want to go or to get involved. Ray asked me if I would do this just for him. I felt rather obligated as he was always doing things for me and so I agreed. I didn't think anything would happen.'

She met Jones and drove with him to the wood a few hours before the crime. She asked him what he was going to do and he told her that the less she knew about it the better it would be for her. Then he suggested she should stay with him so she would know he was not going to harm Mrs Cook, but she said she did not want to stay and he drove her back to her home.

'Mr Cook rang me at 4.30 pm next day,' she went on. 'I knew he had been involved in an accident because somebody told me and I bought a local paper. When Cook rang I asked if he had been injured and he said he was all right apart from his ankle and a bump on his head. I asked about Mrs Cook and he said, "Oh, um . . ." and I thought he was crying. Next day, a Saturday, he came to see me and he was very upset and did not want to talk about what had happened.'

After Mr Cook's arrest she saw Jones and asked him how he had killed Mrs Cook. Eventually he told her he had hit Mrs Cook with a car jack and warned her that she had better not tell the police. 'He did not actually say he would kill my mother, but said my mother was always on her own, and I took it that he would. It was very, very frightening.'

Cross-examining the witness about her association with Raymond Cook, Mr Gibbens asked: 'The whole aspect was that you had to have money in order to keep on living with him and you could not get money without the removal of Mrs Cook?' 'That is not true,' retorted Miss Newell. 'I did not know about his financial affairs.'

'Would you agree that throughout the time you knew him Mr Cook was a sort of silent lumpkin who did as you bid him?' – 'No, no: not throughout the time.'

'Is it true that you frequently told people you were toughening up Cook?' – 'I told this to Jones once.'

'What were you toughening him up for?' – 'As Mr Cook said, he had no self-confidence.'

Asked about Cook's relationship with his wife, Miss Newell said she thought he was fond of his wife. She didn't suppose a man could live with a woman for seven years and have two children if he wasn't fond of her.

Mr Gibbens: 'Notwithstanding he was living with you and getting you pregnant, was going to have his wife abducted, get a divorce and marry you?' – 'We did not talk about marriage.'

Mr Justice Stable thumped the bench as he asked her: 'Well, what *did* you want?' 'I didn't mind if he went back to his wife or not,' retorted Miss Newell.

Mr Draycott asked the witness if, from her knowledge of Cook, she thought he would have taken his wife into the wood if he had known she was going to be harmed. 'No,' replied Miss Newell.

Mr Draycott: 'But you are suggesting that Cook was the prime mover in the arrangements with Jones and that you were on the sidelines?' – 'Yes.'

'A reversal, I suggest, of the true position? – 'No.'

When Miss Newell again denied knowing what Jones was going to do to Mrs Cook, Mr Justice Stable asked her: 'You are saying all these negotiations were going on behind your back?' 'They must have been,' she replied.

Summing up for the Crown, Mr Gibbens said that Miss Newell was the one who provided the motive and means while she kept safe and sound behind the scenes. 'There have been women in history who have done that. Lady Macbeth got her husband to commit murder while she remained aside. Like Lady Macbeth, this woman was urging her lover to "screw his courage to the sticking place." He was in her grip. Cook thought it was for marriage and love. She thought of nothing except money.'

Mr Gibbens told the jury that in Miss Newell they had seen a baffling psychological problem. 'In the witness-box she presented herself to you with a wide-eyed innocence, but does she finish up as such an innocent maiden as at first she seemed? You may think you have seen a very clever, very ruthless and dangerous woman . . . Cook is in love with her still and has shown some effort not to put the blame on Miss Newell. What sort of morality does this woman have? What sort of truth do you think she worships? If her evidence is right she was not interested in marriage or Cook. She was out for money.'

During the judge's summing-up, on the thirteenth day of the trial, Valerie Newell sat crying in the dock, but she gave no sign of emotion when the jury, after a three-hour retirement, found both her and Cook guilty as charged.

Commenting, 'It is in my discretion to pass the same sentence in each case,' Mr Justice Stable said that he was sentencing them both to imprisonment for life. He commended the police team which investigated the murder, making particular reference to PC Sherlock – 'but for whose intelligence this car accident might have escaped further investigation.'

On 9 August 1967, seven weeks after she was sentenced, Kim Newell gave birth to a 6 lb son, who was christened Paul. Her father stated that the baby would be adopted so that he would never know his background. Five months later the Court of Appeal dismissed applications for leave to appeal by both Valerie Newell and Raymond Cook.

By one of those 'stranger than fiction' coincidences, an earlier attempt to make murder appear to be a road accident was also thwarted by an astute and observant police constable. Like PC Sherlock in Oxfordshire, PC William Kevan, whose beat included the Gorbals slum area of Glasgow, refused to accept at its face value the too obvious evidence before him.

He saw the bloody and mangled body of a woman lying in Prospecthill Road on the outskirts of the city. She had been found by taxi driver John Kennedy as he was on his way to Glasgow from Kilmarnock at 12.55 am on 28 July 1950; he thought that she had been struck by a heavy lorry travelling at speed.

His telephone call for help brought Constable Kevan to the scene. The woman was obviously dead and she had, equally obviously, been killed by a vehicle because tyre marks were visible on the body. But there was something very odd about the marks. They were quite distinct but they were not parallel – and at one point they actually crossed each other. Further along the road PC Kevan found more tyre marks indicating that a car had turned on the grass verge running alongside.

Constable Kevan became suspicious. He was also very puzzled – by what he failed to find! As an experienced traffic officer he knew that when a car or lorry hits a pedestrian with the violence evident in this case the impact almost invariably does some damage to the vehicle, shattering glass or at least chipping the paint. He dropped on to his hands and knees. In the brilliant light of the patrol car's headlamps he went over every inch of the road. He found nothing, not even the pieces of dried mud which are normally dislodged from the underside of any vehicle involved in such an incident. The constable contacted the CID and Detective Chief Inspector Donald McDougall decided to treat the 'accident' as a case of murder.

The suspicions of the police were quickly justified by the findings of forensic experts. Professor Andrew Allison and Dr James Imrie, who performed the post-mortem examination, announced that they had never seen a road accident victim with the type of injuries sustained by the woman in the case. There were thirty separate external wounds as well as severe internal injuries, but only superficial grazing on the legs. When a person is knocked down by a vehicle the legs are usually struck by some part of the car, but there was nothing on this woman's legs to indicate an impact that might have thrown her to the ground.

There were two more sinister discoveries. Some of the injuries, including a crushed pelvis, had been inflicted after

32

death – and there was a large bruise on the right temple which did not match up with the other crushing injuries. It appeared to have been caused by a blow from a blunt instrument.

On the medical evidence it looked as if the woman had been knocked out by a blow to the head, placed on the road while still unconscious and had then been run over twice – once while she was still alive and a second time after death. An examination of the tyre marks ruled out the possibility that she had been killed by one vehicle and run over by a second car while lying dead on the road. All the tyre marks matched exactly and all had been made by the same car, travelling first one way and then, after turning, from the opposite direction.

There was nothing on the murdered woman to identify her, but the police attempts to name her were swiftly ended by Mrs Rose O'Donnell, of Rutherglen Road, Glasgow. She called at a police station during the morning of 28 July. Mrs O'Donnell was worried because her friend, Catherine McCluskey, had failed to collect her two children, six-year-old Patrick and baby John Anthony, aged three months, whom she had left with Mrs O'Donnell the previous evening. The woman told a police officer that she had looked after the children on previous occasions when her friend, an unmarried mother, wanted to enjoy an evening out, but never before had Miss McCluskey failed to collect the children and take them to her home in Nicholson Street.

It soon became plain from Mrs O'Donnell's description of the missing woman – aged forty, blonde, wearing a red coat and white shoes – that she was the woman who had been found in Prospecthill Road a few hours earlier. Later that day Mrs O'Donnell identified Catherine McCluskey's body at the city mortuary and just as she was leaving – almost as an afterthought – she said: 'She told me she was going out with a bobby who's on point duty in the Gorbals.'

Further information linking the dead woman with a police officer was given by Mrs Grace Johnstone, a neighbour in Nicholson Street. She informed detectives that Miss McCluskey had told her that the father of the elder boy was an American and the baby's father was a policeman who was going to pay her maintenance. Miss Jean Dickson, a clerical officer with

33

Glasgow Assistance Board, stated that Catherine McCluskey had applied for assistance after the birth of her second child. At the time she had refused to name the father but eventually admitted that he was a policeman who was sometimes on duty near her home.

It was not difficult to trace the wanted man. At a period when a Glasgow constable's wage was only between six and seven pounds a week very few of them were able to run a car, but one who was known to use a large black Austin was one who had also been on the duty roster for the night of 27–8 July. He was James Ronald Robertson, aged thirty-three, a handsome, dashing, athletic man, married and the father of a boy and a girl.

During the week of the murder Robertson had been working with PC Dugald Moffatt, who recalled that at 11.15 pm on 27 July Robertson had left his beat after saying, with a wink, that he was going to take a blonde home. Robertson went off in the Austin car, registration number DYS 570, in which he had arrived for duty that night. Moffat did not see him again until 1.10 the following morning, when he noticed that Robertson was soaked with sweat, untidy and dusty. The truant officer explained his unkempt state by saying that the exhaust pipe of the car had broken and that he had had to tie it up with string.

Before examining Robertson's car, which was kept in a garage in Gorbals Street near his home in Hillingdon Road, Glasgow, detectives made a routine check of the registration number, and were amazed to find that it had been issued to a farmer in Aberdeenshire for his tractor. The car itself had been stolen some months previously from a solicitor in Lanarkshire. Robertson, when questioned on these points, admitted quite frankly that he had found the car abandoned, had failed to report it, and had then changed its number plates for some he had taken from the tractor. He had since been using the car.

On his own admission he was a thief. But was he also a murderer?

The car was examined by Sergeant Colin McCallum, of the Traffic Department. The body of the vehicle was undamaged and showed no sign of having struck anything or anybody, but on the underside there were traces of blood, skin and hair. The exhaust pipe was broken. McCallum had previously looked very carefully at the road surface where the woman's body was found and had noticed some odd little scrape marks near the tyre impressions. He took the Austin back to the murder scene and was able to prove that these scrapes had been made by the broken exhaust pipe touching the ground as the car went over the body.

Robertson, who had been in the police force only five years – he had previously been an inspector in the Rolls-Royce aero-engine factory in Scotland – was arrested while he was on duty on the night after the murder. He admitted at once that Catherine McCluskey had been killed by the car he was driving, but insisted that it had been an accident. He said that he had known the woman for about a year, since going to investigate a disturbance at a house at which she was living, but denied that they were on intimate terms and rejected emphatically the suggestion that he was the father of her baby. On the night of 27 July he had met her casually and she had told him that she had been turned out of her lodgings. She had asked him to drive her to a village some miles away. He said that he had refused because he was on duty and could not be absent from his beat for so long, but he agreed to take her to some friends who lived nearer. In Prospecthill Road they had an argument and he told her she could get out and walk. She left the car 'in a huff' and he started to drive away, then thought better of it and reversed the car with the idea of picking her up again.

Suddenly, he said, he felt a bump and noticed a sharp increase in the exhaust noise. When he got out of the car he found the woman lying partly underneath it. He tried to pull her clear, but could not do so because her clothing was caught in the propeller shaft. He returned to the car and moved it backwards and forwards several times in an attempt to free her. When he succeeded she was lying on the road and he suddenly realized she was dead. Overwhelmed by the hopelessness of the situation, he got back into the car and drove away.

It was, of course, an incredibly stupid story. It was amazing that Robertson had any hope that anyone would believe it. Even the most dim-witted learner driver would scarcely have tried to free an injured person by driving the car backwards and forwards over the victim. How much less likely that a tough Glasgow policeman, with considerable experience of road accidents, should perform such senseless manoeuvres! If the constable's story was true he would only have had to report the accident and help would have been immediate.

In fact he did report the 'accident', but not quite in the terms he used afterwards. On 3 August, five days later, another police officer opened the report journal in Cumberland Street police box and there found this entry: 'At 2.30 a.m. to-day, July 28, a woman was knocked down and fatally injured in Prospecthill Road near Aikenhead Road. Motor-car, believed to be a small blue Austin, maybe 10 h.p., was driven by a man wearing a light fawn Burberry coat. The car did not stop and was last seen driving citywards in Aikenhead Road.' The report was signed by James Ronald Robertson.

When arrested he was found to be carrying a heavy rubber truncheon – not part of the regulation equipment of a policeman on the beat. There was further damning evidence, too, in the lack of bloodstains on his uniform or shoes. In view of the mangling injuries to Catherine McCluskey it was obvious that no one could have touched her without some transference of blood, yet microscopic examination failed to reveal even the tiniest spot on Robertson's clothing.

His story about the woman's clothes becoming entangled in the propeller shaft also collapsed. At Glasgow High Court, where he was tried for murder before a jury of eight men and seven women in November 1950, an Edinburgh consulting engineer, Mr Charles Wicks, pointed out that the shaft in the Austin was enclosed. 'I don't see how it was possible for her clothes to become entangled in this manner,' he said.

During the six-day trial two pathologists described their findings. Mr John (later Lord) Cameron, for the defence, said that a small dent in the rear bumper of the car could have been caused by the impact of a human bone. Professor John Glaister, the famous medico-forensic expert, agreed that such a dent could be caused in that way, but added, 'It would produce a definite and extensive bruise and such a bruise was not

36

one of the woman's many injuries.' The professor told the court, 'I can account for most things by a forward running down on more than one occasion. . . . I am forced to the conclusion that the body must have been completely relaxed and in a recumbent position when the car first struck it.'

A possible motive for the murder was suggested by the Crown counsel, Mr H. Leslie, KC, who submitted that there was a bond between Robertson and Miss McCluskey which he was trying to break and she was attempting to maintain, but Robertson, throughout his trial, insisted that the relationship between them was no more than a casual one. No one will ever know the truth about that because the jury decided, by a majority vote, that Robertson was guilty of murder. He was hanged at Barlinnie, Glasgow, on 15 December 1950.

But one thing is certain. Had he not made the mistake of running the car twice over the woman – presumably to make sure that she was really dead and could never give evidence against him – he would not have been suspected of involvement. The double set of tyre marks provided the first clue and led to a chain of forensic evidence which eventually sent him to the gallows.

Although 'murder by car' is a comparative rarity, murder faked to look like accidental death has been tried many times and in many ways, and in the days before the evidence of forensic scientists was accepted as an aid to detection it was probably often successful. But a killer who tries to disguise a murder as an accident nowadays, no matter how calculated his planning and how unlikely his weapon, has to be clever indeed to outwit the 'laboratory detectives'.

Another man who mistakenly thought he had found the perfect means to kill was Kenneth Barlow, a thirty-eight-year-old trained nurse. In 1957 he was working at St Luke's Hospital, Huddersfield, Yorkshire, and the weapon he chose to help him was insulin. Used in the treatment of diabetics and in psychiatric wards, this substance cannot be found chemically after death. None the less, scientists were able to prove that the victim had been given a massive dose of insulin, and as a result Barlow gained the doubtful distinction of being the first person in Britain to be tried and convicted of murder by this means.

Barlow was married twice. His first wife, Nancy, aged thirty-three, died in hospital on 9 May 1956, leaving him with a ten-year-old son, Ian. Some inquiries were made into her death, which occurred after a very short illness, and on 15 June 1956 an inquest was held by Manchester City Coroner, Mr R. S. Bishop. Recording a verdict of death due to natural causes, Mr Bishop said: 'After the most thorough investigation there is no reason to suppose that this lady died from unnatural causes. Although the doctors are in some doubt as to the precise cause of death, it seems that the balance probably is in favour of this rare disease, encephalitis.' (Encephalitis is a virus infection of the brain commonly called 'sleepy sickness' because unnatural sleepiness is one of the symptoms.)

On 30 June, two weeks after the inquest on his first wife, Barlow married Elizabeth, a vivaciously attractive, dark-haired nurse, aged twenty-nine, who was also employed at St Luke's Hospital. The couple set up home in a small, semi-detached house in Thornbury Crescent, Bradford, where they were regarded by the neighbours as a very happy and devoted couple.

At 11.20 on the night of 3 May 1957, ten months after their marriage, Kenneth Barlow was hammering on the door of the adjoining house, calling, 'Get a doctor quickly.' When his neighbours, Thomas Skinner and his wife Ann, went into Barlow's house they found Elizabeth Barlow lying in the bath, apparently unconscious. A doctor arrived ten minutes later and certified death.

Detective Sergeant John Naylor of Bradford CID was called to the scene just after midnight. He noticed that the water in the bath had been run off, that there was no moisture on the rug or linoleum, and that the sleeves of the pyjamas worn by Barlow were quite dry. The husband told the officer that his wife, who was eight weeks pregnant, had had fish and chips for her midday meal and had then done some housework and washing. After a 5 pm meal of toast, grapefruit, bread and butter and tea she had gone to bed at about 6.30, but had asked to be called at 7.30 to watch television. She decided, however, to stay in bed and at 9.20 called her husband upstairs because she had been sick. After attending to his wife, Barlow also got into bed. Later his wife complained of being too hot, removed her pyjamas in the bedroom and went to have a bath. He stayed in bed, reading, but dozed off to sleep. When he woke some time after 11.0 he was surprised to find that his wife had not returned. He found her lying under the water in the bath, so he removed the plug and tried artificial respiration by pressing her abdomen.

The woman's body was left undisturbed in the bath until Dr David Price, pathologist, arrived at 3.30 the following morning – and noticed a number of very odd features.

Mrs Barlow was lying on her side with one leg drawn up, the fingers on one hand were loosely curled round the other wrist, and the general impression was of a person in a natural sleep. There was no sign of violence, no evidence of splashing, nothing to indicate that she had fallen under the water. There was still some warm water caught in the crook of one elbow.

The pupils of her eyes were so widely dilated that it was impossible to discern the colour of the iris, which was no more than a faint line. The obvious conclusion was that she had been unconscious before death by drowning and that whatever had caused her to lose consciousness had also been responsible for the dilation of the pupils and for the earlier sweating and sickness. It seemed possible that the woman had become hypoglycaemic – developed a low concentration of sugar in the blood – but a post-mortem examination showed no evidence of any disease which could have caused this condition spontaneously. As insulin is given to reduce the high concentration of sugar in the blood of a diabetic, it appeared probable that Mrs Barlow, who was not diabetic, had been injected with insulin, which had had the result of lowering the blood sugar level so drastically that it had caused unconsciousness.

Support for this theory came when a second examination of the woman's body – made with the aid of a hand magnifying glass – revealed four tiny puncture marks in the buttocks. But theory was one thing – proof was another. Barlow felt certain that proof would not be forthcoming and, secure in that knowledge, he left Bradford and moved to Newton Way, Edmonton, North London.

He had not reckoned on the painstaking skill of the medical scientists who, in the months following the drowning of Mrs

39

Barlow, were to make hundreds of tests in an attempt to determine whether or not insulin had been present in her body at the time of death.

Because the police laboratories were not licensed to make the experiments necessary in this case – involving the use of mice, rats and guinea pigs – the tests were made at the biological assay division of Boots Pure Drug Company Ltd. A crude extract prepared from buttock tissue removed from the dead woman was injected into more than a thousand mice. These injections caused convulsions and the rodents which were allowed to die were found to be hypoglycaemic. Those that were given injections of glucose, which is used to increase the blood sugar level in cases of insulin coma in human beings, recovered from their convulsions and regained consciousness. Other tests on rats and guinea pigs bore out the theory that insulin was present in Mrs Barlow's body.

While the scientists were busy in the laboratories, detectives were pursuing their own inquiries about Barlow and found that he had revealed an interest in insulin more than once and had made some extremely strange remarks on three occasions. Between Easter 1954 and Christmas 1955 he had worked at Northfield Sanatorium, Driffield, Yorkshire, where he had looked after some diabetic patients who required insulin treatment. During this period he had explained to a nursing orderly, Mr Harry Stork, details of the different types of insulin and the reactions of one type against another. He then said to Mr Stork, 'You could commit the perfect murder with insulin. It cannot be traced because it disappears into the bloodstream.'

Nurse Joan Waterhouse, who was a student nurse at the East Riding General Hospital when Barlow worked there early in 1954, said that he told her, 'You could kill somebody with insulin as it cannot be found in the body unless it is a very large dose.' Mr Arthur Evans, a former patient at Northfield Sanatorium, told the police that Barlow once remarked when referring to insulin, 'Get a load of this and it's the quickest way out.'

On 26 July 1957, nearly three months after Elizabeth Barlow's death, her husband was interviewed in London by Detective Chief Superintendent P. Cheshire and Detective Inspector

E. Lockley; he at first said that he had no idea how hypodermic syringe marks had come to be found on his wife's body. After further questioning, however, he broke down and cried and said that he had given her six injections during a period of two weeks, using ergometrine (a drug made from a fungus which attacks rye grass, and is sometimes used in early pregnancy cases where the foetus has died) in an attempt to bring about an abortion.

He told the officers that his wife had kept pleading with him to get her something from the hospital, saying that she would put her head in the gas oven rather than have a baby. She was terrified when she knew she was pregnant because, although she wanted a child, she was frightened that the birth might kill her. She used to lie awake at night crying bitterly and eventually he stole six ampoules of ergometrine from St Luke's Hospital, where he was working at the time. He gave her the sixth injection after dinner on the day she died.

Chief Superintendent Cheshire said to him: 'From information supplied to me I believe that insulin was injected into your wife.' Barlow replied: 'That would have killed her. . . . I gave her ergometrine, only a small quantity each time. I did not use insulin. I am not responsible for Elizabeth's death.' He did not know that the first analysis on specimens removed from the body at the post-mortem examination had consisted of a search for several hundred poisons and drugs – including procaine, quinine and ergometrine – and that no trace of any of these substances was found.

Barlow was arrested and charged with murdering his wife. When he appeared before Mr Justice Diplock at Leeds Assizes in December 1957, the Solicitor-General, Sir Harry Hylton-Foster QC, prosecuting for the Crown, described it as 'an unusual and interesting case' – and certainly one of the unusual features was his own opening speech. 'Barlow and his wife were to all outward appearances a happy and devoted couple and he was greatly distressed when she died,' said Sir Harry. 'You may come to the conclusion that he had determined she should not bear the child she was then carrying, but apart from that factor there is no sort or kind of reason outwardly why he should have desired her death. Apart from what science has discovered since she died, there would be virtually nothing that would justify the accusation that he murdered his wife by injecting her body with insulin.' He submitted, however, that tests conclusively established that Mrs Barlow's body had contained insulin and that there was no question of it reaching her body otherwise than by injections.

In most murder cases in which scientific evidence is introduced it is put forward either to corroborate or disprove other evidence, often tipping the balance one way or the other. In the case of Kenneth Barlow it was plain from the first moments of his trial that the charge would stand or fall on the results of the work of the 'laboratory detectives'. Not surprisingly the greater part of the five-day trial was taken up by the evidence, examination and cross-examination of the scientific witnesses.

Dr Alan Currie, senior scientific officer at the Forensic Science Laboratory, Harrogate, said that he had carried out tests which eliminated the possibility of Mrs Barlow's death being caused by ergometrine, any common poisons or by any of the medicaments found in the house. 'There is no practical chemical test to detect insulin in these circumstances,' he said. 'You cannot test for insulin itself. You test for its effects.'

Dr Alan Price expressed the opinion that Mrs Barlow had died of asphyxia due to drowning while she was in a coma following an overdose of insulin.

'Is it possible for you to say that insulin is proved to have been in the body?' asked Mr Bernard Gillis QC, for the defence.

Dr Price said that there was no scientific proof that the substance received by analysis was insulin in the sense that they had isolated the chemical and could produce it, but the substance they had investigated had all the properties of insulin. 'Extracts produced the effects of insulin and substances which affected insulin affected the extracts,' he said.

In reply to further questions by Mr Gillis, Dr Price said, 'So far as I know this is the first time there has been an investigation of this order.'

'So if anybody else is charged in similar circumstances he may have the advantage of more established scientific knowledge than this man has, this being the first occasion?' – 'I hope so.'

42

The judge asked Dr Price if Mrs Barlow could have given herself the injections. The doctor replied that, in view of the position of the puncture marks, it was very unlikely.

When Mr Vernon Birkenshaw, of Boots' biological assay section, said that tests on extracts from Mrs Barlow's body tissue showed that the substance extracted was of an insulin type, he was asked by Mr Gillis if he was able to determine which type of insulin. He replied 'No, sir.' Another Boots witness, Mr Sydney Randall of the biochemistry section, told the court that three experiments he had conducted pointed to the fact that the extract from Mrs Barlow's body was insulin. Cross-examined by Mr Gillis, he said that he could not definitely exclude adrenalin from the crude extract he had prepared from the woman's body tissue, but he thought its inclusion extremely unlikely.

Barlow, in the witness box, denied emphatically having given insulin to his wife. 'I was more deeply in love with her when she died than when she became my wife,' he said. There had never been any unhappiness between them. He did not want her to have the child any more than she wanted it, but he was reluctant to do anything to endanger her life.

Asked by the Solicitor-General what exactly he did when he found his wife in the bath with her head under the water, Barlow replied: 'I am sure I tried to pull her out. I pulled the plug out of the bath. I was almost demented at the time. I tried artificial respiration and fell into the bath and scrambled out.'

'Someone will wonder how it was there was some quantity of water held up in her right elbow. Can you think how that came about?' – 'I did not notice. I do not know how it could have happened.'

'If she was lying on her back while you were giving her artificial respiration it is difficult to see how that could occur.' – 'I do not know.'

Asked why he had made a statement to the police in which he had omitted reference to the fact that he had been injecting his wife with drugs, Barlow said that he knew that the ergometrine had no bearing on her death. He added: 'I was attempting to make a new life and it seemed to me if I was to be arrested and charged with stealing ergometrine, and possibly charged with aiding and abetting an abortion, I had lost my career completely.' He said there was no possibility of him mistaking insulin for ergometrine.

Dr J. A. Hobson, acting physician in charge of St Luke's Woodside Hospital, London, was called for the defence and put forward a theory that the insulin found by the tests could have been generated within the woman's own body. In a state of emotional anxiety, such as fear, the body secreted adrenalin which increased the blood sugar, and at the same time secreted insulin, often in large amounts. 'If for some reason the woman knew she was slipping down and drowning in the bath, she would be terrified,' he said. 'I think that would produce all the symptoms the chemists have described.'

Dr Price, recalled by the prosecution, said that if this theory was correct the insulin would have been evenly distributed, but this had not been the case.

Cross-examining Dr Hobson, the Solicitor-General said that eighty units of insulin had been found in 170 grammes of tissue. Bearing in mind the body weight of the woman, this would mean that, if it came from the natural pancreas, Mrs Barlow would have had 15,000 units of insulin in her body.

'This is quite impossible, is it not?' – 'Not quite impossible. There is the question of the different selectivity of tissues.'

Mr Gillis submitted that there was no direct evidence that insulin had been injected into Mrs Barlow's body on the day of her death or any other day. There was no evidence that Barlow or Mrs Barlow had ever been in possession of insulin. Referring to the 'gossip and chatter' of nurses who alleged that Barlow had spoken of insulin as a means of murder, Mr Gillis asked: 'Is it supposed that in 1954, before he knew the dead woman, he was planning murder? Was he an ogre planning to murder a woman he had not yet married?'

The jury was out for an hour and twenty-five minutes before returning a verdict of guilty. Sentencing Barlow to life imprisonment, Mr Justice Diplock said: 'You have been found guilty of a cold, cruel and carefully calculated murder which but for a high degree of detective ability would never have been found out. Those responsible for the scientific research which led to the detection of this crime are to be very highly congratulated for the skill and patience they have devoted to their public task.'

In the Court of Criminal Appeal on 24 March 1958 the Lord Chief Justice dismissed Barlow's application for leave to appeal.

3

Secrets beneath ashes

Murder by fire – murder in which fire is the actual instrument of death – is a rare method of killing, but quite a number of people have used arson in an attempt to eradicate evidence of the greater crime, no doubt in the belief that the flames would destroy not only the victim but any clues which might incriminate the killer.

One of the very few cases in which fire was the primary weapon of murder was the notorious Arthur Rouse affair. This licentious Lothario of travelling salesmen had, by the time he was thirty-six, become so enmeshed in a web of extra-marital sex (he was said to have seduced eighty women and to have fathered countless bastards all over the British Isles) that he decided on disappearance as the only way out.

His blazing Morris Minor car, containing a charred and unidentifiable body, was found in Hardingstone Lane, a turning off the Northampton to Stony Stratford road, at 2.0 in the morning of 6 November 1930. Ownership of the car was established and the victim was naturally assumed to be Rouse, who lived most of the time with his legal wife – there were other bigamous ones – in Buxted Road, Finchley, London N12. That assumption might well have continued had not Rouse, with incredible stupidity, decided to visit another of his 'wives', who was about to give birth to a baby of which he was the father. By the time he arrived at her bedside in Wales the evening papers were already carrying the story of his 'death' in the blazing car.

Rouse was arrested and charged with the murder of an unknown man, found guilty at Northampton Assizes and hanged on 10 March 1931. The victim was never identified. He was at first believed to be a hitch-hiker and later, the more likely explanation, a tramp.

But Arthur Rouse was an exception. Many killers have started fires *after* murders in the hope that the deaths of their victims will appear accidental. A classic example of this latter type of crime was another 'body in a car' murder which hit the headlines in 1933, three years after the Rouse case. But this time there was no mystery about the identity of the victim. The only question to be answered was: Who was the killer?

The setting for this story – one of love, hate and passion – was a large and lonely farmhouse called Saxton Grange, in Towton, near Sherburn-in-Elmet, in the West Riding of Yorkshire. The owner, Frederick Ellison Morton, aged twenty-eight, was a farmer who ran a business known as Cattle Factors Ltd, dealing in the selling of cattle and horses on hire-purchase. His wife, Dorothy Louise, daughter of a textile manufacturer from Huddersfield and the same age as her husband, was not a conventionally pretty woman, but had a slim, elegant figure – enhanced by the expensive and well-cut clothes she wore – and was well endowed with that indefinable something known in those days as sex appeal.

The couple had a two-year-old daughter and employed quite a large staff on the farm, including a girl called Ann Houseman. She was a companion-help to Mrs Morton. Another employee was Ernest Brown, a thirty-five-year-old groom. At the time of the tragedy he was employed as an odd-job-man.

Outwardly, the household and business appeared to be normal, happy and well ordered. But beneath the surface there was a simmering cauldron of discontent, jealousy and fear. Morton was a hard-drinking man frequently out late at night and often away from home on business trips. Mrs Morton was a keen horsewoman and when Ernest Brown was first employed as a groom the two were naturally together a good deal. He was a powerfully built, arrogant, good-looking man. She was an attractive woman neglected by her husband. They became lovers and for three years maintained a sexual relationship – by mutual desire according to Brown, but under threats of violence if Mrs Morton was to be believed.

The relationship changed early in 1933 when Dorothy Morton found another lover, and throughout that spring and summer, instead of sneaking out of the house to join the groom, she was driving off to Wetherby, about fifteen miles away, to see the other man whenever her husband was away. Fred Morton appeared to be unaware of his wife's infidelities, but Brown knew quite well that he had been supplanted, and lost no opportunity to make life difficult for his ex-mistress. He was critical, too, of the manner in which his employer was running the business. He objected to the way Morton treated customers who were unable to keep up hire-purchase agreements, and had been heard to say that they would all be out of work unless Morton changed his methods.

He became so disgruntled with the whole situation that in June 1933 he flew into a rage when Morton told him to mow the lawn. Brown protested that it was not a groom's work. Morton retorted that if he didn't like it he could 'take his cards'. Brown left the farm in a huff, but a few days later was back. He told Mrs Morton that her husband was to reinstate him 'or else' – and the woman, frightened by his threats, persuaded her husband to re-employ Brown. Morton made it plain that, as a replacement groom had already been engaged, Brown was to be no more than a handyman about the place.

So the summer lengthened. Dorothy Morton avoided her ex-lover as much as possible, keeping Ann Houseman near her whenever there was likely to be an encounter, and departing for fresher delights at Wetherby as often as she could. Ernest Brown became more and more jealous, vindictive and gloomy. Fred Morton, apparently untroubled, continued to spend most of his free time with his drinking cronies.

Then, on 5 September that year, Morton was away from the farm all day and Brown went out to deliver a cow. When he returned he asked Mrs Morton if she had been out and she replied: 'Yes.' He shouted at her: 'Where have you been?' When she told him that she had been bathing with a man friend, Brown was so enraged that he pushed her into a cowhouse and caught her by the throat. She screamed for Ann, but when the girl appeared Mrs Morton told her there was nothing the matter. She said that she had only been calling a cow.

The two women went into the house. Brown followed them and asked Mrs Morton to go out with him to help get the ducks in. She made some excuse and Brown left the house.

At 9.30, about half an hour later, the women heard a noise like a small explosion. Ann rushed to the kitchen, where she found Brown. He told her that he had been shooting rats. Again he went out, but constantly returned to the house during the evening. He said very little but appeared to be rather drunk and wild-eyed.

Soon after 9.30 the telephone rang and when Mrs Morton answered it she was disturbed to see Brown lurking in the hall. A few minutes later he was back in the kitchen, where he took a white-handled game knife from a drawer and left without giving any explanation. The two women were thoroughly frightened by now and their terror mounted when he returned with a shotgun. The situation was sinister but he stayed only long enough to clean and reassemble the weapon – again in total silence.

Morton had been expected home by about 9.0 pm and in fact he had left a public house at Tadcaster, only four miles away – quite sober – at 8.15. Mrs Morton and Ann waited for him in a state of mounting panic, convinced by that time that Brown intended to kill one or both of them. Their hopes of welcoming Morton as their protector died when the ex-groom came into the kitchen at 11.30 pm and told them that Mr Morton had returned to the farm but had immediately gone out again. Too frightened to go to bed, they locked themselves in the bathroom and watched for signs of Morton's return. They did not see a car draw into the farm, but they noticed Brown crossing the yard in the direction of the back door, to which he had a key. There was the sound of footsteps and creaking on the stairs – mysterious noises which continued for about an hour. When all was quiet the two women went into Ann Houseman's bedroom, but no sooner had they done so than there were more sounds of stealthy footsteps and other unidentifiable noises. It was 2.0 am before the house was silent, but there was no question of sleep for the terrified women. They just watched and waited.

They did not know what they expected to happen but both were overtaken by a peculiar dread. At 3.30 am there was a loud explosion. Almost immediately the whole sky was lit up by flames leaping high from the garage. Forgetting their fear of Brown, Mrs Morton and Ann rushed downstairs to telephone the fire brigade. The line was dead! They snatched the little girl from her cot and ran out of the house. Dashing through the darkness, they crouched in a hedge as they saw Brown approaching. He did not see them and they left their hiding-place to run half a mile across the fields to the village of Towton.

By the time they had reached friends, Brown had called out the farm bailiff, Mr Murray Stewart, who had a cottage nearby. The two men went back to the farm after calling the brigade. Stewart noticed that Brown was fully dressed, and wearing a collar and tie. When he looked into the ex-groom's room over the stables he saw that the bed had not been used that night.

Firemen arrived to find the garage and some of the barns a mass of flames. In the cold light of dawn firemen and police officers examined the gutted buildings. They found the burnt-out wrecks of two cars, a Chrysler and an Essex. Lying across the front seats of the Chrysler, face downwards, were the almost completely cremated remains of a human body. From the grisly relic Police Constable John Broadhead removed a bunch of keys, a pocket knife and a small piece of material with a button attached – virtually all that remained to identify Frederick Ellison Morton!

At that stage there was no reason to suppose that his death in the fire was other than accidental, but his killer had not reckoned on the skill of pathologists and forensic scientists.

Making a routine examination of Morton's remains, pathologist Dr P. L. Sutherland discovered nineteen gun pellets and a cartridge wad in the charred flesh. Two pellets were in the heart. Mr Robert Churchill, of the famous London firm of gunmakers, said that the pellets and wad corresponded with those from a cartridge case which had been picked up in a field at Saxton Grange, and the cartridge case was fired from the left-hand barrel of a gun found at the farm. This gun, he said, was not liable to accidental discharge. It was his opinion that the shot that had killed Morton had been fired when the gun was almost touching the body.

The burnt-out cars were examined by Mr Clifford Bottomley, a Leeds motor engineer. He told detectives that the drain plug of the Chrysler's petrol tank was missing and could have been removed only by using a pair of pliers. The draining plug of the petrol tank had also been removed from the Essex car and among the debris in the garage Mr Bottomley found a spanner which exactly fitted this plug.

Detective Chief Superintendent William Blacker, head of West Riding CID, made a detailed search of the area in which Brown was supposed to have been shooting at rats, but found no trace either of pellets or of pellet marks.

Post office telephone operators reported that there had been no reply to calls put into Saxton Grange after 9.40 pm on 5 September, and Julius Whitehead, a post office linesman, told the police that the telephone wires outside a window at the farm had been cut.

Morton had obviously been murdered and, equally obviously, Ernest Brown was the chief suspect. But the clinching evidence was really provided by Professor Frederick Tryhorn, of Hull University, a leading expert in the behaviour of metals. He took the white-handled game knife which, according to Mrs Morton and Miss Houseman, had been removed from the kitchen by Brown, and saw that its blade looked smooth and sharp. But when it had been microscopically photographed and the pictures had been enlarged many times, a clear pattern of serration was revealed. The cut ends of the telephone wire were photographed and enlarged in the same way. A comparison of the blade and wire ends showed that each little notch and every tiny indentation matched precisely. There was no doubt that the knife had been used to sever the wire.

Questioned by Chief Superintendent Blacker, Brown said that on the night of the fire Mr Morton drove up to the farm at about 11.30 but did not get out of the car and told Brown that he was going out again. Brown left him and heard him 'shunting the car about'. 'I went to bed about 11.45 and never heard the car again,' continued Brown. 'I was awakened by a noise like an explosion about 3.30 am and saw flames over the pigeon cote. The garage was in flames. I released the horses and cattle.' Brown elaborated on this story when, charged with the murder of Frederick Morton, he stood in the dock before Mr Justice Humphreys at West Riding Assizes in December 1933. He declared that Morton was drunk upon his arrival home on 5 September and was annoyed because he

(Brown) had not been able to deliver the cow he had taken out that day. Brown added that earlier that evening he had taken a knife from the kitchen to cut an old head-rope from one of the horses, but he used a black-handled one, not the white-handled game knife.

Both Mrs Morton and Brown were questioned about the relationship between them. Dorothy Morton, dressed all in black, admitted that they had been lovers. 'Then I began to dislike the man,' she said. 'I made it clear that I disliked him and he became very threatening.'

Mr G. H. B. Streatfeild (for Brown) asked her: 'Do you say that for three years this man was threatening to have intercourse with you against your will?' – 'Yes.'

'Did you ever make any suggestion to your husband to get rid of this man who was making your life a torment?' – 'I did my utmost.'

She was questioned by Mr Streatfeild about another man in her life and agreed that she and this man had been surprised in an embrace in the nursery at Saxton Grange. 'Is there not some other person who has succeeded Brown in the relationship Brown once had with you?' – 'I have been intimate with one other man.'

Brown maintained that the relationship between Mrs Morton and himself had been a mutual one and denied that he had ever used force or threats to get her to have sexual intercourse with him. In reply to Mr C. Paley Scott KC, for the Crown, Brown said it was quite untrue that he hated every man who came between himself and Mrs Morton.

He denied having shot Morton, or setting fire to the garage, or cutting the telephone wires. He had not the slightest idea how Morton had met his death. 'Is there anyone of whom you have any suspicions who might have cut the telephone wires?' asked Mr Paley Scott. 'I do not know,' replied Brown. 'Is it your idea that some lover of Mrs Morton's who disliked her husband shot him and set the place on fire?' – 'It may be.'

The widow, too, was cross-examined about this unnamed 'other man'. 'Do you say no other man came into the house that night?' asked Mr Streatfeild. 'Some man, of whom you are fond and who is not fond of your husband?' Mrs Morton said that nobody, except Brown came near the house that night.

The judge: 'If you are putting it that there was a particular person, and one who can be identified, you ought to put the name to her.' Mr Streatfeild: 'It is impossible to do that.'

'If you can identify him, Yorkshire, and if necessary all England, shall be searched to find him and bring him here.' – 'That is impossible. It is just a theory, a possible man in the house, but I cannot identify him.'

This theory was elaborated by Mr Streatfeild in his final speech for the defence. Brown, he said, had no motive for murder. It was not a case of a lover seeking to get rid of a husband so that he could afterwards marry the widow. But if there remained some other person in Mrs Morton's affections there would be a motive for that person to get rid of the husband. The facts were consistent with some other person coming to the farm that night. Some other person could have shot Mr Morton, returned to the house with the gun, which he had seen Brown using earlier, and then deliberately fired the garage after soaking the body with petrol. 'If Mrs Morton had suspicions that her lover had designs on her husband, that would account for her terror,' continued Mr Streatfeild. 'If that assumption is true it is consistent that Mrs Morton, with the frailty of human nature, suspecting someone else of whom she was fond, would not scruple to put the blame on someone she loathed. When love has turned to hate there is no knowing to what lengths that loathing may drag one.'

The jury did not accept the defence theory. They took an hour and ten minutes to find Brown guilty of the murder of Frederick Morton. His appeal was dismissed and he was hanged at Leeds Jail on 6 February 1934.

Brown's expressed fears that his employer was ruining the business were ill-founded. Morton left £18,709 – all to his widow.

Both Rouse and Brown were thoroughly businesslike in their attempts to cover their crimes by fire, and were defeated only because they failed to realize the advances that had been made in forensic science even in the early 1930s. Others have had the same idea but, lacking the intelligence to plan ahead, have used fire more as a desperate afterthought than as a preconceived part of the weapon of murder.

One such case occurred in 1954.

It was 1.0 am on 29 July when an agitated woman, speaking little English, rushed to a car near Hampstead underground station in North London, and told the occupants, a Mr and Mrs Burstoff, that there was a fire in a house in which some children were sleeping. The couple hurried to the house in South Hill Park, Hampstead, NW3, but could see no sign of fire until they opened the French windows leading into the garden and there, on the steps, saw the still smouldering body of a woman, naked except for her briefs.

Mr Burstoff telephoned the police while his wife tried to get some sense out of the woman who had summoned them, but all that could be understood was, 'Me smell burning. Me come down. Me pour water, but she died.' When the police arrived they found that the dead woman was Mrs Hella Dorothea Christofi, thirty-six-year-old German-born wife of Stavros Christofi, who worked as a night-club waiter in the West End of London, and that the woman who had called for help was her Cypriot mother-in-law, Mrs Styllou Pantopiou Christofi.

Those were the bare facts which covered a domestic situation of considerable tension. Stavros had come to England from Cyprus in 1937, when he was just over twenty, and four years later married Hella, who came from a mining town in the Ruhr district of Germany. They had three children, Nicholas, aged eleven at the time of his mother's death, Peter, aged ten, and eight-year-old Stella; they had lived throughout the thirteen years of their married life at the house in South Hill Park. Hella was a gay, attractive, dark-haired woman of thirty-six, fond of clothes and always smartly dressed, efficiently combining her role as housewife and mother with a well-paid job in a London fashion house. It was a happy, well-ordered prosperous family group – until Stavros's fifty-three-year-old mother arrived from Cyprus in July 1953.

Inevitably there were clashes. The younger woman was smart, modern, educated, and it is doubtful if she ever wanted her mother-in-law in the house. Mrs Styllou Christofi, who had come to Britain because her husband in Cyprus was unemployed, had been married at fourteen and had lived the

54

simple life of a peasant. She was by no means a sophisticated woman in her own country and in Britain, with its different language and, to her, strange way of life, she was almost illiterate. Because of her small, bent body and dark wrinkled skin she looked nearer seventy than fifty-three. The older woman was jealous of the fine life her daughter-in-law was leading and did not approve of her wardrobe of smart clothes and shoes, nor of her cosmetics or of the time she spent on taking care of her appearance.

They might have been more tolerant of each other had they been able to communicate, but the woman from Cyprus spoke and understood only her native language and Hella was an English-speaking German. Within a few weeks of her arrival the husband sent his mother away to live with someone else. She returned to South Hill Park after a few weeks, but again there were clashes. Between July 1953 and the summer of 1954 the older woman departed and returned three times, with the domestic situation worsening on each occasion. Hella reached such a state of nerves that her husband arranged for her to take the three children on a visit to her parents in Germany. She was due to make this trip at the beginning of August. Stavros made it plain to his mother that she would have to go back to Cyprus as soon as Hella and the children returned from their holiday.

This was the point of crisis reached by the night of 28 July, when Stavros was at work and the two women and three children were left in the house. Exactly what happened is something that will never be known, but at 11.45 pm a next-door neighbour, Mr John Young, took his dog into the garden and noticed a glow from the garden next door. He called to the occupants and, receiving no reply, looked over the fence. There he saw what he took to be a wax model lying outside the French windows. The arms were raised and bent at the elbows like those of a shop-window dummy and the figure was lying in a circle of flames. There was 'a strong smell of paraffin and burning wax'. He could see into the brightly lit kitchen of the Christofis' house and noticed someone moving about. After a few seconds Mrs Christofi senior stepped outside the French windows and bent over the figure, apparently stirring up the flames. Mr Young, convinced that it was only rubbish being burned, returned to his house and retired to bed.

It was more than an hour later that Mrs Christofi rushed into the street to get help and 1.15 am on 29 July before the police were called. It was immediately obvious that the death of the daughter-in-law was not accidental. There were bloodstains in the kitchen – although some attempt had evidently been made to clean up. Beside the body, which had a wound at the back of the head, were the remains of paper and wood which had been soaked in paraffin. Round the woman's neck there were marks consistent with strangulation and in the dustbin detectives found three pieces of charred material, part of which was still tied in a noose.

Dr Francis Camps, the eminent pathologist, found that the woman had a fractured skull, which could have been caused by contact with the ash plate of the boiler in the kitchen. She had, however, died from strangulation by a ligature. It was established that the pieces of material found in the dustbin were part of a scarf and there was a clean cut through the fabric as though it had been freed from the woman's neck with a knife. The body was badly charred. The only unburned parts were those in direct contact with the ground. It was Dr Camps's opinion that paraffin had been poured over the body while it was lying where it was found.

After the discovery of the body Mrs Christofi was questioned by Detective Inspector Robert Fenwick about what had happened that night. She replied: 'I wake up, smell burning, go downstairs, Hella burning. Throw water, touch her face. Not move. Run out, get help.' Later, with the assistance of an interpreter, she made a statement in which she said: 'When I went to bed Hella and I were on perfectly good terms. She said she was going to do some washing, but I do not know if she meant clothes or whether she was going to wash herself. Every evening she washes the whole of her body with water. I got up at 12.55 am and saw smoke. Hella was lying on the floor of the yard. I saw little flames at the ankles, around the knees, on both arms. . . . I put some water in a bowl and splashed it over her with my hand, then I get some more water and threw it over her.' Shown the remains of the scarf taken from the dustbin, she said, 'I was so afraid I did not even notice anything round her neck.'

Hella's wedding ring, which she never removed from her finger, was missing from her dead body and was later discovered, wrapped in a piece of paper, tucked behind an ornament in her mother-in-law's bedroom. Questioned about this, Mrs Christofi said that she had found the ring on the stairs and kept it because she thought it was a curtain ring.

She was taken to Hampstead police station and told by Detective Superintendent Leonard Crawford that she would be charged with the murder of her daughter-in-law. She denied any knowledge of the killing and added: 'I did not make use of any paraffin, but some days previously some paraffin was spilt on the floor. I did not pay any attention to it, but stepped on it, and possibly the smell was the result of that. I know nothing more.' It was a pitifully inadequate explanation and she evidently realized it, because she had a different story to tell when she stood before Mr Justice Devlin and a jury of ten men and two women at the Old Bailey in October 1954. She then said that she had heard the voices of two men downstairs after her son had left for work on the evening of the murder. Later she saw two men, one of whom was carrying a suitcase, standing in the yard outside the house. She knocked at the door of Hella's room, but there was no reply, and when she went downstairs she found her daughter-in-law burning outside the French windows.

The jury did not believe her and she was sentenced to death. Ten Members of Parliament, led by Sir Leslie Plummer, asked for a retrial on the grounds of a medical report made by Dr Thomas Christie, principal medical officer at Holloway Prison.

This report, dated 5 October 1954, stated: 'The clinical picture is that of a non-systematized, delusional mental disorder. In my opinion, the fear that her grandchildren would not be brought up properly induced a defect of reason. . . .' Dr Christie formed the opinion that Mrs Christofi was insane, although medically fit to plead and to stand trial. The defence at the trial had not raised the issue of insanity because the accused woman refused to plead guilty but insane. She had instructed her counsel not to mention Dr Christie's report.

The Home Secretary, Mr Lloyd George, decided not to intervene and Styllou Christofi was hanged at Holloway on 15 December 1954.

She may have been insane, but she knew what she was doing – it was later revealed that she had previously been tried for the murder of her mother-in-law. This trial had taken place in Cyprus in 1925, when she was twenty-four years of age. She and two other women were charged with killing the mother-in-law by ramming a burning torch down her throat, but all three were acquitted.

An even more ineffectual attempt to cover murder by fire was made by the killer of two elderly spinsters in South-West London on 29 August 1959. The women, eighty-eight-year-old retired school teacher Elizabeth Caroline Ivatt and her companion-help, Phyllis May Squire, aged sixty-four, lived in a ground-floor flat at Chesham Court, Trinity Road, Wandsworth, SW19. A quiet, respectable and intelligent couple, they were well liked by their neighbours and seemed the most improbable people to become the victims of a murderer.

It was certainly the last thought in the minds of neighbours who saw smoke coming from the windows of their flat on that summer afternoon, and firemen who arrived after the tenants of other flats had failed to get any response to their calls had at first no reason to believe that it was anything other than an accidental fire. The whole flat was full of smoke and there was what appeared to be a bundle of burning rags on the floor in Miss Ivatt's room. Closer inspection, however, revealed that the smouldering bundle was the body of Miss Squire. She had been savagely beaten about the head and her face was covered by a pillow. Miss Ivatt was dead in her bed – killed not by fire but by a fracture of the skull. It was evident that the two women had been murdered – a chair with two legs broken was the weapon used – and that the fire had been started in the hope that the flames would consume the evidence. Papers, blankets, cushions and some wooden coat-hangers had been soaked in paraffin, but the fire had smouldered rather than blazed and had been quite ineffectual in its purpose.

It was an apparently motiveless murder and the killer was not difficult to trace. He had previously called at the flat to answer an advertisement for someone to look after Miss Ivatt on Miss Squire's weekly free day and he had returned that afternoon for further discussions. He was seen by a number of people and was soon identified as Ronald Herbert Benson, aged thirty-four, an unemployed clerk living with his parents at Nottingham Road, Upper Tooting, London SW17.

'It couldn't be me, could it?' he replied when questioned by Detective Chief Inspector Leslie James. 'You know I wouldn't do a thing like that normally, but I am really two persons and my other self in one of my attacks could.' After further interrogation Benson said that the old ladies had given him a cup of tea. He asked them for money, but they said they couldn't help, so he 'went and hit the old lady'. He readily admitted having started the fire.

It was plain that the man was mentally unbalanced. During the war, while on civil defence duty, he had been blown from his bicycle by a bomb explosion and had since suffered from epileptic fits. Twice he had attempted to commit suicide. He was charged with the double murder and was committed for trial, but by the time he appeared at the Old Bailey in October 1959 his mental state had deteriorated so much that he was found unfit to plead and was sent to Broadmoor.

4

Remains without names

Although the principal activities of forensic scientists engaged in murder cases are usually directed towards identifying killers or allying them to crimes – and sometimes this work establishes the innocence of suspects – it is also occasionally their gruesome task to determine the identities of victims. The murderer of an unknown person is rarely caught, because identification is the first brick in the edifice of the investigation and without it the police have no foundation on which to build. For this reason a number of killers have mutilated the bodies of those they have slain, and some would have evaded detection but for the remarkable skill of pathologists and forensic scientists.

Scientists have found it possible to construct fairly accurate pictures of dead persons even in cases where there has been extensive dismemberment or when death has occurred so long before the discovery of a body that nothing but a collection of bones has been left for examination.

The approximate height of a victim can be calculated from any of the longer bones of the legs or arms. Even one tooth can give a good clue to age, as can quite small sections of head bones. Sex can be determined not only from pelvic bones but from breast bones, the skull (the walls of the cranium are normally thinner in men than in women), and sometimes even from the upper arm joints and thigh and shin bones.

In cases where the identity of a dead person is suspected it is possible to 'match up' some facial characteristics by super-imposing an enlarged photograph of the head in life on to a photograph of the skull and then printing the two negatives onto one piece of paper. Plaster casts of feet can be fitted into the shoes of a missing person. Identity is confirmed if the toe and heel marks in the shoe match indentations in the casts.

For the murderer to eliminate the identity of the victim is not as simple as it may seem to the layman, even when the killer is a skilled anatomist like Dr Buck Ruxton, central figure of a classic case of the thirties.

Ruxton, an Indian whose real name was Bikhtyar Hamim, practised in Lancaster, where he lived in Dalton Square with his thirty-five-year-old mistress, Isabella Van Ess (known as Mrs Ruxton) and the three children of the alliance. They had been together for some years, but quarrelled furiously and he decided to get rid of her.

Mrs Ruxton and her maid Mary Rogerson, a girl of twenty, were last seen alive on 14 September 1935, when they were supposed to have left Lancaster for a holiday in Edinburgh. Two weeks later most of their remains – two skulls, two trunks, three breasts, seventeen parts of limbs and forty other pieces of flesh – were found scattered in a ravine near Moffat, Dumfriesshire in Scotland.

The doctor had been painstaking in his attempts to prevent identification. Mary Rogerson's eyes had been removed because she was known to have a bad squint. Mrs Ruxton had ugly legs, of uniform thickness from her knees to her feet, so part of the soft tissue had been sliced away to give an appearance of shapeliness.

His efforts were in vain. A team of pathologists equally painstakingly reassembled the horrible pieces of these human jigsaws and were able to say without doubt that the reconstructed bodies were those of Mrs Ruxton and Mary Rogerson. The older woman had been strangled and the girl – believed to have been killed because she was a witness to the first murder – had a fracture of the skull.

Ruxton cockily denied all knowledge of the crime, but bloodstains were found in the bathroom at the house in Dalton Square and fragments of human tissue were still trapped in the wastepipe of the bath. He thought he had been clever. But he was not quite clever enough. He was hanged at Strangeways Jail, Manchester, on 12 May 1936, at the age of thirty-seven.

Detectives recalled the Ruxton affair when the torso of a woman was found in an olive-green suitcase at Wolverhampton, Staffordshire, on 5 April 1968. The case had been left under the table of a second-class coach on the 10.40 am Euston to Wolverhampton train. It was taken to the left-luggage office where an attendant, Mr Leslie Stevens, noticed blood oozing from the seams.

The torso, with arms but minus head and legs, was wrapped in green curtain material and was dressed in a pale blue, floral-patterned tunic, pink cardigan and blue, hand-knitted sleeveless pullover.

Detective Superintendent (now Commander) Roy Yorke and Detective Sergeant George Atterwill, of Scotland Yard, were called in by the Midlands police. Scarcely had they arrived in Wolverhampton than a message from Essex police sent them hurrying to Ilford. Another suitcase, this time containing a pair of female legs, had been found on the banks of the River Roding.

Both torso and legs appeared to belong to an Asian woman and the detectives formed the theory that the killer had thrown the case containing the legs from a train travelling from Ilford to Liverpool Street station in London, and had then gone on to Euston, carrying the other case with the torso, to board the train for Wolverhampton.

Roy Yorke, one of the Yard's most brilliant investigators, immediately launched a massive hunt for a third suitcase which he believed would contain the missing head. Frogmen searched the bed of the River Roding and a helicopter was used to scan the whole of the railway track from London to Wolverhampton. The train from Euston had stopped at Rugby, Coventry and Birmingham and a careful check was made of all suitcases and bags deposited in left-luggage offices at those stations. Between 150 and 200 passengers had travelled on the train and they were all asked to identify themselves. Taxi-drivers and car-hire firms were requested to contact the police if anyone of them recollected a fare carrying an olive-green suitcase. When I visited Roy at Ilford he disconsolately told me that the result of all these inquiries was precisely nil.

He was then forced to rely upon pathologists and forensic scientists, working in the laboratories at Guy's Hospital, London, for a word-picture of the woman – from the torso and legs. They decided that she was a girl aged between seventeen and nineteen, less than five feet in height and weighing only about six stone. At the age of twenty-five the vertebrae, the skull and other bones reach the stage of maximum development – known as ossification. In the case of the dismembered girl, this stage had not been reached. Sandal marks and callouses on her feet indicated that she had only recently started wearing European shoes, so had presumably not long been in this country. The medical team's outstanding work revealed that she had been pregnant, but had lost the baby either by abortion or miscarriage. Further tests disclosed that her pubic hairs had been shaved within twenty-eight days of death – supporting the theory of a recent abortion or miscarriage.

It was on 7 May, one month after the discoveries of the torso and legs, that Mrs Maureen Rice, wife of an Epping Forest worker of Blake Hall Road, Wanstead, Essex, opened her door to a rather agitated man. He said to her: 'I picked up a bag which looked better than mine, but there's a head inside. Will you call the police?'

The blue duffle bag containing the head had been tucked under some bushes on Wanstead flats – part of Epping forest – and Mrs Rice recalled having first seen it there about three weeks previously.

The head, with black hair, fitted the torso. The 'laboratory detectives' found another clue – a filling in a tooth that was not the work of an English dentist. It was later established that the filling had been done by a Delhi dentist.

The girl was evidently an Indian and, from discussions with religious leaders, Roy Yorke concluded that she was a Moslem, Sikh or Hindu. But about ten thousand such women had entered Britain in the past two years. Identification on such slight evidence seemed almost impossible.

The investigating team plodded on and their real break came when knitting experts in Britain failed to recognize the pattern of the hand-knitted pullover which had been found on the torso. It was not possible, they said, to obtain such a pattern in this country. Detectives had the pullover photographed and displayed large pictures of it at Indian and Pakistani clubs, Sikh temples, airports and all railway stations. With the pictures was a message, in three dialects, appealing to anyone who recognized the pattern to contact the police.

Nine Indian women came forward with the same information – that the pattern was a traditional one unique to Jullundor and neighbouring villages in the Punjab. Detectives made a further check of immigration records and found that two thousand women from that part of India had been among the ten thousand who had arrived in Britain in the past two years. Yorke and Atterwill, operating in Wolverhampton and Ilford, launched yet another breakdown of the figures. They established that of the two thousand only about one hundred girls were under the age of twenty.

The laboratory experts advanced a theory that a scar on the girl's left leg could have been made for a blood transfusion after an abortion or miscarriage. Inquiries were switched to hospitals. At Barking General Hospital in East London detectives found records of a nineteen-year-old Indian girl named Sarabjit Kaur, a native of the Punjab, who had reported to the hospital in November 1967, only two months after her arrival in Britain, for confirmation of pregnancy. She had never returned.

Detectives went to this girl's address at Fanshawe Avenue, Barking, and asked to see her. They explained that it was part of a check going on all over the country and they wished to see her passport. Her father Suchnam Singh Sandhu, denied that she was in Britain, saying that he had only two daughters with him. This was known to be untrue because immigration records showed three. The two other daughters were known as Kaur, and Roy Yorke discovered during this part of his inquiries that all Sikh women call themselves Kaur, while the men retain the family name – in this case Sandhu. (Since this mammoth murder investigation, immigration officials have insisted upon the women entering their family names on their passports.) The father lied again by saying that he had no photograph of her. Detectives saw one in the house and also found a physics textbook which, when examined by fingerprint experts, revealed prints matching those taken from the dead girl.

Detective Superintendent Yorke, Detective Sergeant George Atterwill and their team back-tracked further on the life of the victim they now knew to be Sandhu's daughter. Their painstaking inquiries revealed that while in Delhi Sarabjit had fallen in love with her cousin, a married man. She had come to England with her family, became a medical student at East Ham Technical College and when her father had discovered that she was still exchanging passionate letters with her lover and that it was possible that he was also coming to England, had run away from home and gone to live in one room. It appears that before her father traced her and forced her to return home, she visited a back-street abortionist who was forced to give her a crude blood transfusion to save her life. In the opinion of the scientists, the scar from the transfusion showed beyond doubt that it had not been carried out by a person medically trained in England.

Thirty-eight-year-old Sandhu, who had been a school teacher in the Punjab village of Jullundor and had brought his family of seven to England in September 1967, was closely questioned by the police and then charged with the murder of his daughter.

At the Old Bailey in November 1968 it was said that Sarabjit had been given thirty grains of phenobarbitone, twice struck on the head with a hammer, and her body was then dismembered with a hacksaw.

The motive for the father's crime was explained by Mr Alastair Morton, for the Crown. He said that Sandhu's main reason for coming to this country was to earn more money so that Sarabjit could study to become a doctor. Soon after the family's arrival in England the father discovered that his daughter was pregnant and the girl had been killed because of the disgrace pregnancy out of wedlock had brought to the family. The father of the expected child was an Indian of 'a lower caste', and this stigma was so great that neither of her other sisters would have found an Indian husband if this had become known.

Sandhu pleaded not guilty and insisted that Sarabjit had commited suicide. He said that she had been to college and then attended the Delhi School of Nursing in India. On 4 April she told him that she had ruined her life and did not want to live any more because a boy she wanted to marry had married another girl. She said nothing about pregnancy and he did not know that she had ever been expecting a baby.

He then went out, leaving her in the house. When he returned he found her lying dead on the floor. There was an empty glass on a table nearby and it looked as if she had struck her head on the sewing machine as she fell. She had left a suicide note, but he had lost it.

The accused man declared that he had intended to tell the police of her death, but on the way to the station he was almost knocked down by a car because he was not looking where he was going, so he thought it would be better if a relative accompanied him. This man persuaded him that it would not be wise to tell the police, so they returned to the house, cut up the body and put it into suitcases. Together they disposed of the two cases and the duffle bag. The relative he mentioned, Hardyal Singh Sandhu, denied in court knowing anything at all about the girl's death and said he had had no part in disposing of the body.

Suchnam Singh Sandhu's story was not believed by the jury. He was found guilty of murdering Sarabjit and was sentenced to life imprisonment. He was refused leave to appeal against conviction.

One point in this tragic story remains unexplained. Sandhu knew that his daughter was pregnant, but did he know that she had subsequently lost the child she was carrying? And had he known, would he have killed her . . . ?

In normal times the discovery of a dead body, wherever it may be found, is immediately a matter for police suspicion. Death can have been due to natural causes, to suicide or accident – but there is always a chance that the answer is murder. During the Second World War, particularly at the height of the blitz in big cities, there was a fifth possible verdict – death by enemy action.

It was not such a rarity for the remains of bodies to be discovered in bombed buildings years later, so that demolition workers getting rid of some of the debris in the wreck of the Vauxhall Baptist Chapel in Kennington Lane, London SE11 on 17 July 1942 were not particularly surprised to uncover a pile of human bones and decayed flesh. More than one hundred people had been killed when the chapel was bombed on 15 October 1940, and during the six months between 1940 and March 1941 a small area of that immediate vicinity had been a target for the *Luftwaffe* on a number of occasions.

It was not the first body that the demolition workers had uncovered. They followed their usual routine in such cases – left the remains as they were found and informed the police. Detective Superintendent William Rawlings and Divisional Detective Inspector Frederick Hatton saw the remains of this supposed raid victim and, again as a matter of routine, arranged for them to be examined by a pathologist – in this instance Dr Keith Simpson in his laboratory at Guy's Hospital.

The head was not attached to the trunk and parts of the arms and legs were missing. The remains were obviously female because the uterus was still intact and enlarged in such a way as to suggest pregnancy.

The ground under the chapel was known to have been a cemetery at some time, the last burial having taken place about fifty years previously. As the body had been in the cellar, could it have been thrown up from the old burial-ground as a result of bomb blast? 'No,' said Dr Simpson. 'Death took place between twelve and eighteen months ago.'

Was it possible that the woman had been one of the 104 victims of the 1940 raid? A check of records showed that the number of bodies found in the chapel tallied with the number of people reported missing by relatives. The police now had one body too many.

An examination of the chapel cellar revealed two anomalies – the presence of a quantity of lime in the soil only at the site of the body and not in any other part of the earth-floored cellar, and the complete absence of any fragments of clothing or personal belongings which could be associated with the woman. She had been naked when she met her death, and her body had been covered with slaked lime.

The inference was obvious and the suspicions of the detectives were confirmed when Dr Simpson told them that the body had not been blown apart by bomb blast but had been amateurishly dismembered after death; that attempts had been made to remove any part of the body which might provide identification; that some efforts at burning the body had been made; and – the clinching evidence – that a tiny bone in the voice-box had been fractured in such a way as to prove that the woman had been strangled.

An ironical twist to the story was that the slaked lime, which the murderer had hoped would destroy the body, actually preserved enough of the remains, including the larynx, to enable the cause of death to be established. Without the lime there would probably have been far greater destruction by rats and bacteria.

So the woman had been murdered. But the police were still left with the twin problem of who she was and who killed her.

Dr Simpson was able to tell them that she was between forty and fifty years of age, a little over five feet in height, and – from a fraction of scalp still adhering to the back of the skull – had dark brown hair turning grey. She had worn a denture, probably with seven false teeth, and had fillings in four of her natural teeth. An X-ray photograph of the uterus yielded one other important clue. The enlargement was not due to pregnancy, but to a large fibroid tumour.

Even with this information the task of piecing together the background of the victim was a formidable one. The police force was inevitably badly understaffed at that time and the population was a shifting one. Many people lost their homes and were forced to move, sometimes several times. Women became 'camp followers' of the members of the armed forces and did not always tell their friends and relatives. Others made sudden decisions to disappear into the heart of the country when the bomb raids on cities became more than they could bear. Others had actually been killed in the raids but were officially 'missing' because there was nothing to prove them dead. Of the thousands of missing girls and women on police files in 1942, at least one thousand were approximately of the same age and height as the murdered woman. The relatives of each of these 'possibles' were seen by police officers, who asked: 'Did she wear a denture with seven teeth?' and 'Was she suffering from a fibroid tumour of the womb?'

They drew blank until they talked to Miss Polly Dubinski, who lived with her aged mother in Shoreditch, East London. Yes, said Miss Dubinski, her sister – reported missing since April 1941 – was aged forty-seven, five feet one inch in height, had dark-brown hair going grey, some false teeth, and had attended two hospitals because she had a tumour of the womb, in each case refusing to have an operation.

68

Police records showed that the woman, Mrs Rachel Dobkin, had been reported missing by her sister because she was separated from her husband, Harry Dobkin, of Navarino Road, Dalston, London E8. Apart from the formal records, detectives had good reason to remember this particular case because of the extraordinary story Miss Dubinski had told them at the time. On 12 April she reported that her sister, then living in one room in Dalston, had failed to return after going to meet her 'no good' husband the previous day. This meeting, declared Miss Dubinski, was against the advice of a medium who, at a seance on 8 April, had told Mrs Dobkin: 'You are planning to go and meet someone. Don't go. I see sadness for you.'

Due note was taken of this information. A few days later Miss Dubinski, by now very excited and worried, was back with a further instalment of her spiritualistic story. She had attended another seance held by the same medium, to whom she had handed a scarf belonging to Mrs Dobkin. The medium had passed into a trance, clutching her throat as though she was choking. Miss Dubinski, determined to learn more, visited a second medium. The second one, again in a trance, declared: 'There is a passing out, a sudden death.'

What, demanded Polly Dubinski, were the police going to do about it?

Largely to satisfy this voluble lady, who minced no words in telling them, 'My sister has been strangled by her husband,' they interviewed the second medium. This woman told them that she had 'seen' Mrs Dobkin in her husband's arms in a small, hot room, and had clutched her own throat to demonstrate how she had seen Rachel's head falling.

On 16 April 1941 detectives interviewed Harry Dobkin, employed at that time as a firewatcher by a firm of solicitors at 302 Kennington Lane, next door to the already bombed Baptist Chapel. He seemed unconcerned by their inquiries and admitted quite frankly that he had met his wife in a café in Kingsland Road, Shoreditch, on the afternoon of 11 April. When they had left the café she boarded a No. 22 bus and told him she was going to see her mother. He had not seen her since.

Dobkin, a Russian-born Jew who had lived in England

since infancy, was equally forthcoming about the history of his marriage. Arranged in Jewish fashion by a marriage broker, it had been a failure from the start and he and Rachel had separated only three days after the ceremony in 1920. On two occasions they had been reunited, but only for a few days. A child had been born nine months after the wedding and for the past twenty-one years Rachel had been after him for payment of the one pound weekly (later reduced to ten shillings) due under a maintenance order made at Old Street Magistrates Court. He had frequently attempted to evade payment, had been fined for falling into arrears and had been to prison for contempt of the court order. The only reason for their meeting on 11 April was Rachel's determination to get some of the money owing to her – and Dobkin's equally firm resolve that she should not get any. He did not pretend to be upset because she had disappeared. So far as he was concerned, it was 'good riddance to bad rubbish'.

There was absolutely no evidence to suggest at that time that Harry Dobkin had killed his wife, or indeed that she had been the victim of any murderer. But the circumstances of her disappearance began to assume a more sinister aspect after Polly Dubinski's description of her sister was compared to that of the reassembled remains found in the chapel cellar fifteen months later. Dr Simpson had reported that there had been some attempt to burn the body before covering it with soil and lime and it was recalled that a rather mysterious fire had been reported in the ruins of the Baptist chapel on the night of 15–16 April 1941, only a few hours before Dobkin was first interviewed about the disappearance of his wife.

It was a small fire in the days when very big fires were all too commonplace, so nobody had attached much importance to it. A constable on patrol duty had reported it at 3.23 am and firemen had doused it without much trouble. Dobkin, whose job as a firewatcher was to extinguish incendiary bombs and call the fire brigade if necessary, told the constable that the fire had started at 1.30 am but he had not bothered about it because it was among rubble in the cellar of an already ruined building. There had been no air-raid in the area that night, so he knew it had not been caused by incendiaries.

One person who was rather more concerned about this fire

was the pastor of the chapel, the Reverend Herbert Burgess. He looked into the cellar soon after the fire and noticed what appeared to be the remains of some old straw mattresses. He was so convinced that someone had started the fire deliberately that he made a note in his diary to that effect.

Dobkin was interviewed a second time in April 1941 because the circumstances of his wife's disappearance were certainly suspicious, but again he emphatically denied all knowledge of her whereabouts. Despite this the police decided to investigate the cellar and detectives spent more than a day digging over the floor. They found a newly dug hole, but there was absolutely nothing in it. Eventually they stopped excavations when warned that any more disturbance would probably cause the whole building to collapse on them.

Rachel Dobkin's name was still on the long list of missing persons; it might well have stayed there indefinitely had it not been for the discovery of the demolition workers in July 1942.

It was clear from Dr Simpson's reconstruction of the body and the description given by Polly Dubinski that the possibilities were in favour of the murdered woman being Mrs Dobkin. Possibility became probability when Miss Mary Newman, in charge of the photographic department of Guy's hospital, matched up an enlarged picture of Rachel Dobkin's head with a photograph of the skull. This technique had been used for the first time in the Ruxton case seven years earlier and, as on that occasion, the matching was remarkably accurate – the picture of the face superimposed on that skull fitted like a mask.

Final identification, however, was provided by a dentist, Mr Barnet Kopkin, who recognized Mrs Dobkin's picture in the newspapers and came forward with the information that he had treated her at his North London surgery from April 1934 to March 1940. He was expecting her to return for further treatment, but she had failed to keep her last appointment. From diagrams he provided, showing an unusual thickening of the jaw ridges and a very high palate, it was clear that this patient was the murdered woman. A replica of the dental plate he had made for Mrs Dobkin exactly fitted the upper jaw of the skull. When Mr Kopkin examined the skull at Guy's Hospital, he was able to say with certainty that the remaining teeth carried his own fillings.

Harry Dobkin was interviewed yet again. This time he was told that the remains of his wife had been found in the cellar of the chapel. 'What cellar?' asked Dobkin. 'I don't know what you are talking about. I don't know of any cellar at the chapel and I don't believe it is my wife.' He had been told nothing of the police suspicions of murder but, in the written statement he volunteered, he started by saying: 'In respect to what you say that my wife had been found dead or murdered. . . .'

He stuck to his story when, charged with the murder of Rachel Dobkin, he faced Mr Justice Wrottesley and a jury in No 1 Court at the Old Bailey in November 1942. Asked by Mr L. A. (later Mr Justice) Byrne if he had been fond of his wife, Dobkin replied, 'No.' Asked at what stage he had ceased to care for her, he answered, 'On the day I got married.' He admitted frankly that when he last saw his wife he had no desire ever to see her again, but was emphatic in his assertion that he did not kill her.

The case for the defence, put by Mr F. H. (later Mr Justice) Lawton, was that the woman in the cellar was not Mrs Dobkin, and that if she was Mrs Dobkin she had not been murdered. Dr Simpson, in evidence, had mentioned a curvature at the top of the spine which he thought had been brought about by an attempt to shorten the body for burial. Questioned by Mr Lawton, he said there were no abnormalities of the bone to indicate that this curvature had been a congenital condition. 'Anyone with that degree of curvature would be a very obvious sight in life, don't you agree?' asked Mr Lawton. 'If it was present in life,' replied Dr Simpson.

'Look at this picture of Rachel Dobkin . . . no one with such a curvature would look like that, would they?' – 'Of course they wouldn't look like that. I have described the curvature as occurring after death. I have examined the neck to establish whether or not the curvature was present in life.'

'If it was present in life, it couldn't be Rachel Dobkin, could it?' – 'It was not present in life.'

'That is not quite what I asked you. If it was present in life it couldn't be Rachel Dobkin, could it?' – 'I am not prepared to consider whether it was present in life. I found clear evidence that it was not present in life.'

Dr Simpson was later cross-examined by Mr Lawton as to the cause of death and asked if the injury to the throat might not have been caused by the woman being flung by bomb blast on to a kerb or other sharp piece of masonry. 'I have examined over eleven thousand cases, but I have never seen such an injury except in manual strangulation,' replied Dr Simpson.

The jury took less than twenty minutes to find Dobkin guilty. He was hanged at Wandsworth Jail on 7 January 1943. Before his execution he confessed to the crime, saying that Rachel was always after him for money and he wanted to be rid of her for good.

Teeth were the final deciding factor in the identification of Rachel Dobkin's remains, but in the case of a child's skeleton discovered under nearly a ton of stones in a moorland gully on the Yorkshire moors, the teeth were the only means of identification.

It was on a fine summer day in June 1968 that Doreen Mary Hepworth, a rather skinny little girl, piquantly attractive with a wide, ready smile, vanished eight days before her eighth birthday. Wearing a pink floral dress, she left her home in Grosvenor Terrace, York, to play in a nearby park. She did not return and was reported missing by her parents, Wilfred and Patricia Hepworth.

Detective Superintendent (now Commander) William Marchant, of Scotland Yard, took charge of the hunt for the child. Every house in Grosvenor Terrace was searched from attic to cellar and police loudspeaker cars toured the town, broadcasting Doreen's description. A police artist painted her portrait in colour and it was displayed outside York police station. Troops were called in to search the moors beyond Ripon, twenty-four miles away, because some people had reported seeing a child like Doreen in that area on 29 June, the day she disappeared. There was not a single clue to her whereabouts.

It was more than three months later, on 3 October that the pathetic remains of a child were found nearly forty miles from Doreen's home, half a mile from the B6265 road, near Pateley Bridge. Soldiers and policemen with dogs had reached within two miles of the remains in their stony grave during the earlier search for the girl!

There was little doubt in Bill Marchant's mind that it was the end of the hunt for Doreen, and confirmation of his suspicions came from Mr Graham Turner, chief dental officer of York education authority. The teeth in the jawbones of the skeleton matched the records of treatment, including a complete list of fillings, that Doreen had received.

Superintendent Marchant also had strong feelings about the identity of her murderer – a man who had lived in the same street as the Hepworths and had been seen giving sweets and pennies to children. This man, a thirty-seven-year-old lorry-driver named James Franklin Cockerham, had been interviewed several times but had always denied any knowledge of the girl's disappearance.

Eventually he confessed. He told Marchant that the child had visited his flat and asked him for sweets, then jumped on to his bed and started swinging her legs. 'All of a sudden I got the impression it was my ex-girlfriend taunting me as she had done before. . . . I remembered no more until I saw the body on the floor.' He said he had trussed up the body and put it into the kitbag of his moped, which he rode forty miles to 'lonely, desolate moorland' and there buried the body.

In a statement, Cockerham said: 'I wish to make it clear I did not sexually assault this child and her death was the result of my losing my temper because I had a sudden vision that she was my former girlfriend.'

When tried for murder at Leeds Assizes in December 1968, Cockerham pleaded not guilty. He said he was sorry and upset for Mr and Mrs Hepworth, but he was innocent. 'I had no intention of killing her. She just flopped over and went limp.'

Mr Henry Scott QC, prosecuting, asked him why he did not rush downstairs from his flat to get help. Cockerham replied, 'I have liked children all my life, but this was the first and only time I had allowed one in my room and then this happened. I was in a panic in case anyone thought there was something wrong.'

'You trussed her up and pushed her in a kitbag?' – 'Yes.'

'And went right through the centre of York?' – 'Yes.'

'When you threw her down that hole and poured the rocks on her, did you know what you were doing?' – 'I have no idea because I was blank at the time. I must have been doing these things but I wasn't consciously doing what I was doing.'

The trial ended with a life sentence for Cockerham after Mr Justice Bridge had ruled that the jury could not return a verdict of manslaughter. In May 1969 Cockerham was refused leave to appeal.

5

Wicked women

Throughout criminal history poison has always been the most popular murder weapon for women. It is simple to introduce during the preparation of food, it involves no force or gruesome mess, like a bloody shooting or knifing, and it does not require the brutal strength involved in strangling or battering a victim to death.

In a period of twenty-four years, between 1934 and 1958, at least three women poisoners who might otherwise have 'got away with it' were brought to justice with the help of 'laboratory detectives'.

The first was Mrs Ethel Lillie Major, until her arrest a quite unremarkable woman who lived a humdrum and apparently respectable life with her husband Arthur at 2 Council Houses, Kirkby-on-Bain, near Horncastle, Lincolnshire. In 1934 they had been married for seventeen years and had one son, Lawrence, aged fifteen. Mrs Major was also the mother of an illegitimate daughter, Auriol, born before her marriage. Auriol lived at nearby Roughton with Mrs Major's father, Tom Brown, a gamekeeper.

Arthur Major, aged forty-four, a lorry-driver, was a powerful, active man who had become a figure of some consequence in local circles. He was a member of the parish council, keen to preserve and improve the amenities of the village. He belonged to the British Legion, taking part in all their local activities, and at the village church he was respected and valued as a sidesman and member of the parochial church council. The Rector of Kirkby-on-Bain, Canon F. M. Blakiston, described him as 'a very decent sort of fellow'.

At home it was a different story. Arthur Major was a drunkard. His wife, two years his junior, undoubtedly suffered a great deal, both physically and mentally. She was often threatened and sometimes knocked about and so was the boy, to whom she was passionately devoted. Rightly or wrongly, she believed her husband to be unfaithful to her. Unlike many heavy drinkers, Major had no periods of remorse, either for his drinking or his violence. The more his wife pleaded with him to stop drinking, the more he drank. He showed no kindness or tenderness to the woman he had once loved – the woman who had changed from a pretty, laughing girl to a plain, haggard drab, looking ten years older than her actual age.

It is difficult to pinpoint the period at which their at first happy married life began to change, but it is certain that in their last few years together they grew to hate each other. Weeks went by without them exchanging a word and for some time they lived separate lives in the same house, with Mrs Major preparing meals for herself and Lawrence, and Arthur Major eating solitary suppers, mostly of corned beef, before embarking on another evening's heavy drinking. The atmosphere in the home became charged with evil as tension built up during the weeks before Major's death. Eventually, Ethel Major and the son lived for most of the time with Mrs Major's father, Mr Tom Brown.

On 1 May 1934 Mrs Major visited Dr G. Armour, of Woodhall Spa, whose patient she had been for three years, handed him two letters which she declared she had found in her husband's bedroom, and commented, 'Now you can understand why I have been ill these last two years.' Mrs Major said that the letters had been sent to her husband by a neighbour. They were addressed to 'my dearest sweetheart' and 'my sweetest lover' and had rows of crosses at the end of each page.

In the first letter the writer said: 'Baroness looks as if she could kill me to-day. . . . I see her watching you in the garden, also Auriol, but I don't care a fig for either of them. Some day I shall be able to show them something . . . that gipsy is coming true, I believe, dear. You will be fed up with me getting so ratty about things, but I expect you get worked up sometimes.' The second letter referred to one written by Major and went on: 'It is lonely, dear, not being able to come out with you tonight. It is so hard so near and yet so far. What a lot we shall have to tell each other when we are together again. Letters are nice, dear, and do so much to soothe our aching hearts, but some day I shall be able to have your arms round me for always and I shall be able to claim you for my own dearest one.'

At about the same time as her visit to the doctor Mrs Major also received an anonymous letter which read: 'You are slow. Don't you know how your husband spends his weekends? He has a nice bit of fluff now. You can catch him easily if you have him watched. From one who knows about him and Mrs B. . . . I hear he's got a little Major now.'

On Tuesday 22 May Arthur Major arrived home from work at about 5.0 pm, apparently fit and well. He prepared tea for himself. Then he started to repair his bicycle. Suddenly he suffered what appeared to be a fit. Dr F. H. Smith, of Coningsby, was called to the house and found Major in bed, evidently in great pain. He could not speak more than a few words and was having frequent spasmodic contractions of his leg muscles. While the doctor was at his bedside he had a convulsion, and all his muscles became stiff. Mrs Major volunteered the information that her husband had eaten a lot of corned beef. Asked if he had had fits before, she replied: 'Yes, at intervals – for a year or two.'

Dr Smith sent some medicine to the sick man, who seemed a great deal better the following day. On the morning of 24 May Mrs Major called at Dr Smith's surgery. She appeared calm and not unduly distressed and said that her husband had had another fit and had died. She added that his attack had happened so quickly that she had not had a chance to send for help.

The cause of death was certified as *status epilepticus* and, armed with the doctor's certificate, Mrs Major called in undertaker John Ellis Sharp and asked him to arrange the funeral for Saturday 26 May. Both the undertaker and Canon Blakiston told her that Saturday was too early and wanted it to take place on the following Monday. Eventually it was agreed to hold it on Sunday afternoon, 27 May.

It might quite well have taken place on the agreed day, and Mrs Major could have remained a free woman, had not the local police received an anonymous letter signed 'Fairplay'. The writer advised them to look further into the death. 'Have you ever heard of a wife poisoning her husband?' asked the mystery penman. 'Why did he complain of his food tasting nasty and throw it to a neighbour's dog, which has since died? Ask the undertaker if he looked natural after death.'

The funeral arrangements were brought to a rapid halt and internal organs of both Major and the neighbour's dog were sent for analysis to Dr Roche Lynch, the Home Office analyst. After carrying out painstaking tests he found strychnine in every organ he examined, 1.27 grains in the man and 0.16 grains in the dog. As some of the poison would have passed through the body, Dr Lynch estimated that the total dose taken by Major was 2–3 grains. The average fatal dose is 1-2 grains. The greater part of the strychnine was found in the stomach, which led to the conclusion that one dose must have been taken shortly before death. The presence of the substance in other organs indicated that a previous dose had been swallowed about two days before death.

A search of Major's home revealed no traces of poison of any kind, but it was discovered that Tom Brown, Mrs Major's father, had bought some strychnine for the destruction of vermin about four years previously. It was kept in a locked box in a cupboard in his bedroom and he always carried the key in the pocket of his wide cloth belt. It looked at first as if Mrs Major could not possibly have had access to this poison – until Brown recalled that he had lost the first key to the box and had been obliged to buy a duplicate. Again the police went through the Major home. This time they found a shabby purse containing a coin wrapped in paper inscribed 'Mother's Penny' – and the missing key.

Ethel Major was questioned by the police and made a number of statements in which she denied any complicity in her husband's death. She told Detective Chief Inspector Young of Scotland Yard that she thought her husband had been poisoned by the corned beef he was continually eating, adding: 'I did not know that he died of strychnine poisoning.' Inspector Young interrupted her to say: 'I never mentioned strychnine. How did you you know that?' 'Oh,' replied Mrs Major, 'I must have made a mistake. I am still of the opinion that he died of poisoning from the corned beef.' She went on to suggest that the neighbour she suspected of having a love affair with her husband had slipped into the house and put the poison into some food in the larder.

She was charged with murder and stood trial at Lincoln Assizes before Mr Justice Charles and a jury of nine men and three women in October 1934. Mr Norman Birkett KC, who defended her, questioned Dr Roche Lynch very closely about his findings of strychnine.

Dr Lynch told him that about forty per cent of deaths due to strychnine were cases of suicide, but he thought it unlikely that the poison had been self-administered in this case. 'I am quite satisfied that there must have been a second dose,' he said. 'On account of the awful agony he would go through, I do not think any would-be suicide would take it a second time, unless he were insane.'

Mr Birkett said that in the medicine Major had taken during the forty-eight hours of his illness there were 26 or 28 grains of opium, and asked Dr Lynch: 'Opium delays absorption of anything into the organs?' 'It may to some extent, with regard to food, but not with regard to poisoning,' was the reply.

'The effect of the strychnine may be delayed because of the presence of opium?' – 'I do not think there would be delay so far as absorption is concerned, but the presence of a narcotic like opium may to some extent delay the convulsive effect.' Dr Lynch added that he entirely disagreed with the suggestion that a dose of strychnine administered on Tuesday might be so slowed up in effect as to make it appear to have been taken two days later – on Thursday. Neither could he agree that the corned beef Major was said to have eaten on the Tuesday could have delayed the absorption of strychnine into the system.

Mr Birkett: 'Do you concede that it is a possibility that a portion of the strychnine was absorbed and a portion delayed?' – 'It might be delayed for a few hours, but not for forty-eight hours.'

'Is there not a possibility that Major was poisoned by opium?' – 'I cannot agree.'

'I suggest that there is no man living who can say of a surety that he did not die of opium.' – 'I give it as my opinion that he did not.'

Mrs Major fainted during the judge's summing-up and had to be carried from the court after the jury returned a verdict of guilty, with a strong recommendation to mercy, and the judge passed sentence of death. Her appeal was dismissed on 3 December 1934, but last-minute efforts were still made to save her. Most of the villagers of Kirkby-on-Bain, Roughton, Haltham and Horncastle signed a petition which was sent to the Home Secretary. Canon Blakiston also wrote to the Home Secretary and so did the Lord Mayor of Hull, Mr Archibald Stark. On the eve of the execution, Mrs Mary Hatfield, a former Hull City councillor, sent this telegram to the King: 'Please support Lincoln jury, which recommended Mrs Major to mercy, by staying the arm of the law and preventing her execution at Hull Prison tomorrow.'

It was all to no avail. Ethel Lillie Major was hanged at 9.0 in the morning of 19 December 1934, as her father, daughter and a clergyman and his wife knelt together in a cottage at Kirkby-on-Bain and sang 'Abide with me'. . . .

If there was a good deal of understandable sympathy for Mrs Major, there was none for the killer of Sarah Ann Ricketts, a widow aged seventy-nine, murdered at Blackpool in April 1953.

Mrs Ricketts had been widowed twice, both husbands having committed suicide, and had two married daughters who visited her only rarely. Perhaps because she was lonely, or possibly because she felt she was no longer capable of looking after herself, the old lady advertised free accommodation to anyone willing to care for her.

Mrs Louisa May Merrifield, aged forty-six, and her third husband, Alfred Edward Merrifield, who was seventy-one, answered the advertisement. Mrs Ricketts was favourably impressed and the couple moved into her bungalow in Devonshire Road, Blackpool on 12 March 1953 and took over the running of the home.

It seems unlikely that she asked for references. If she had she might have discovered that Mrs Merrifield had served a prison sentence for the illegal possession of ration books during the war, and that in 1947 her three children – one a baby less than a year old – had been taken away from her and placed in a home after being found to be in need of care and protection. The daughter of a Wigan coal miner, Louisa May had been first a mill-hand and then a cook before she married iron worker Joe Ellison in 1931. There was a post-mortem examination when he died in October 1949, but death from 'natural causes' was recorded after it had been decided that he had died from a liver complaint. Within three months she had remarried. Her second husband was a retired mine manager aged eighty, Richard Weston. Three months after the wedding Louisa May was once more a widow, Weston having died of a heart disorder. His pension died with him and there was no money left for his widow. She swiftly looked around for husband No 3 and found Alfred Merrifield. The couple were married on 19 August 1950 – less than a year after the death of the first of Louisa May's three husbands.

Merrifield was a widower and the father of ten children. He had little money and the couple lived on his State pension and help from the National Assistance Board, supplemented by occasional earnings from caretaking jobs and domestic work. Whatever her other shortcomings, Mrs Merrifield was efficient in the house and kept the bungalow in Devonshire Road both clean and comfortable. She must, too, have been a woman of considerable personality because after only twelve days of the new domestic arrangement Mrs Ricketts instructed her solicitor to draw up a new will, leaving the bungalow to Mrs Merrifield. A few days later this was amended to make Alfred Merrifield a joint beneficiary and the revised will was executed on 31 March 1953.

On 9 April that year Mrs Merrifield went to the surgery of Dr Burton Yule at Warbeck Hill Road, Blackpool, and asked him to examine Mrs Ricketts with a view to issuing a certificate that she was mentally fit to sign a will. She said she thought Mrs Ricketts might die a sudden death and she (Mrs Merrifield) did not want any trouble with the relatives. She did not say anything about Mrs Ricketts being ill and when the doctor called at the bungalow Mrs Ricketts was very surprised to see him. He was not asked to examine the old lady with a view to her general heath, but he could see nothing wrong with her and she appeared to be a very healthy woman for her age.

On 13 April Mrs Merrifield called at Dr Yule's house to pay him what was owed for that visit, but said nothing to the doctor about Mrs Ricketts being ill. On the same day Mrs Merrifield visited Dr Albert Victor Wood in Blackpool and asked him to see Mrs Ricketts as she was seriously ill and had been 'for some time'. When Dr Wood said he would call next day, Mrs Merrifield asked, 'What happens if she dies during the night?' Dr Wood called that evening and found the old lady in much the same health as she had been when he had visited her three years previously. She had suffered from a mild form of bronchitis for a long time but otherwise was in good health.

At midday the following day, 14 April, Dr Wood's partner, Dr Ernest Page, went to the bungalow in response to a message from Mrs Merrifield and found Mrs Ricketts very ill. When he made a second visit two hours later the old lady was dead. Dr Page refused to issue a death certificate and Mrs Merrifield protested, 'She has been dying since we came to the place.' Dr Yule was also called by Mrs Merrifield, but he too refused a death certificate.

In spite of this the by now anxious Louisa went two days later to see Mr George Johnson, a Blackpool undertaker, and asked for Mrs Ricketts to be cremated at once. She told him that Mrs Ricketts had said she did not want to be buried with her two husbands because they had both committed suicide, and neither did she wish her two daughters to be told of her death. In the meantime a post mortem revealed that Mrs Ricketts had died of yellow phosphorus poisoning, and that the poison had been administered in one large dose or several small doses on the night of 13–14 April. With the phosphorus was a quantity of bran, the two ingredients being in the same proportions as in Rodine, a rat poison.

Some extraordinary evidence then came to light – evidence, from several different sources, that Mrs Merrifield had been telling people of Mrs Ricketts' death during a period of three weeks *before* the death actually took place. When Mrs Jessie Brewer, of Warley Road, Blackpool, read a newspaper obituary which gave the date of Mrs Ricketts' death as 14 April, she telephoned the police to check whether or not this was a printer's error. She recalled an incident on 11 April when Mrs

Merrifield said to her: 'We are landed. I went to live with an old lady and she died, and she has left me a bungalow worth £4,000.'

As far back as 26 March, Mrs Merrifield told an old friend, Mr David Brindley: 'I have had a bit of good luck. Where I have been living an old lady has died and left me her bungalow.' On 12 April, as she was leaving the house of Mrs Veronica King, of Yorkshire Street, Blackpool, Mrs Merrifield said she had to go 'to lay the old lady out'. Mrs King, more than a little surprised, asked if the old lady was dead. Mrs. Merrifield replied: 'Not yet, but she soon will be.' Even more remarkable was an encounter with Mrs Elizabeth Barraclough, of Livingstone Road, a stranger with whom Mrs Merrifield got into conversation in a bus queue on 13 April. Mrs Merrifield said that she had been to Wigan and when she returned to the bungalow she found her husband in bed with Mrs Ricketts. She added: 'If it goes on again I shall poison the old – and him as well. She is leaving a bungalow between me and my husband, but he is so greedy he wants it all on his own.'

All the evidence pointed to the Merrifields, at least to Louisa, but it was difficult to imagine why she would have taken the enormous risk of murder to get what she was likely to inherit, quite legally, within a comparatively short space of time. Mrs Ricketts was nearly eighty, Louisa Merrifield was only forty-six . . . surely she could have afforded to wait?

It was not long before the police discovered that she could *not* afford to wait. It transpired that Mrs Ricketts, having made the impulsive decision to change her will on the strength of twelve days with the Merrifields, had begun to have second thoughts.

On 13 April – the day before her death – Mrs Ricketts answered the door when George Forjan, of Ascot Road, Blackpool, driver for a firm of wine merchants, called to deliver a bottle of brandy. For some time Mrs Ricketts had been having a bottle of rum once a week and a dozen Guinness once a month, and in the previous six months Forjan had also twice delivered a bottle of brandy. On this occasion she apparently couldn't find any money to pay for the brandy and said to

Forjan, 'I don't know what they are doing with my money. I cannot pay you again.'

Mr Merrifield suggested that he should go to the bank and find out for Mrs Ricketts how much cash she had in her account and, in front of the delivery man, she said that while he was out he could also go to the solicitors because she wanted to change her will. She said to Forjan: 'They are no good to me. They will have to go.'

This man's story to the police, like those of the people who had been told of Mrs Ricketts's death before it actually occurred, was another link in the chain of evidence against the Merrifields – but it was a slender link which needed to be fortified if the guilt of either or both of them, strongly suspected, was to be proved.

Phosphorus had been found in the body, but how had it got there? A painstaking search of the bungalow revealed no containers which might have held the poison, no traces on any cutlery, crockery or cooking utensil. Who had taken it into the house and, even more puzzling, how had a healthy old lady been persuaded to eat or drink anything laced with this strong-tasting, evil-smelling stuff? Some very thorough police work brought answers.

Detectives all over the North of England scoured chemists' shops to find out who had bought tins of Rodine within the relevant period. It was a tedious task, but it brought results. In a Manchester shop a girl assistant named Mavis Atkinson remembered selling a tin of Rodine to an elderly man, wearing a hearing aid, who was accompanied by a woman. She failed to recognize the woman as Mrs Merrifield, but positively identified the man as Alfred Merrifield.

The next act of the drama was played out in the North Western Forensic Science Laboratory, under the direction of Dr J. B. Firth, who conducted a series of experiments to establish how effectively the smell and taste of the rat poison could be masked. Dr G. B. Manning had performed the post mortem on Mrs Ricketts and had successfully identified the phosphorus-bran mixture as Rodine. He led a team of 'tasters'. Each tried the poison mixed with a number of different foods and drinks. The 'tasters' held the mixture in their mouths for a few seconds and then spat it out. Brandy disguised the onion and garlic taste, but the smell still persisted. Rum effectively masked both taste and smell, and so did blackcurrant jam.

At about this time Mrs Alice Hand, of the Promenade, Blackpool, came into the investigation when it was discovered that she had been looking after a handbag belonging to Mrs Merrifield. Mrs Hand had put the bag into a cupboard at her house after Mrs Merrifield had told her, on 15 April, that the old lady had died and that she didn't want Mr Merrifield 'rooting about' in the bag and finding some insurance policies. Mrs Hand had, in fact, previously looked after such policies for Mrs Merrifield because Mr Merrifield had complained that they could not afford the premiums and had threatened to burn them. When the contents of the bag were examined it was discovered that it contained, in addition to the insurance papers, a dessert spoon coated with a sweet, gritty substance. This spoon was rushed to the forensic laboratory, where a staff chemist, Mr Alan Thompson, analysed the contents. As phosphorus evaporates rapidly when exposed to air, it was no surprise that tests for the poison proved negative. But the residue on the spoon was such that it could have been formed had rat poison been mixed with rum.

It was nothing definite, but it was another suspicious circumstance, and the sum total of the whole was enough to justify the arrest of the Merrifields. Their eleven-day trial at Manchester Assizes opened on 20 July 1953. Mr Justice Glyn-Jones presided and sat with an all-male jury. Sir Lionel Heald QC, the Attorney-General, appeared for the prosecution and Mr Jack di V. Nahum for the defence.

There was a considerable conflict of evidence as to the cause of death. Expert witnesses called by the prosecution maintained that it was due to phosphorus poisoning, but an equally expert witness for the defence asserted that the death had been a natural one. This witness was the eminent pathologist Professor J. M. Webster, director of the Home Office Laboratory at Birmingham. He expressed the opinion that, although poisonous phosphorus was found in Mrs Ricketts, she had died from necrosis of the liver.

Asked by Mr Nahum if he attached any importance to the fact that no free phosphorus was found in any of the organs except the intestines and stomach, Professor Webster replied: 'I do. Without the presence of free phosphorus in the other organs one cannot state that death was due to phosphorus poisoning.'

Mr Justice Glyn-Jones: 'Does this mean that, by coincidence, this old lady died so quickly after swallowing phosphorus that it had no time to enter her body?' Professor Webster: 'That is correct.'

The judge: 'Would you express an opinion as to how phosphorus entered the body?' – 'I think it entered by mouth.' In reply to further questions from the judge, Professor Webster said Mrs Ricketts could have ingested phosphorus between fifteen minutes and five hours before she died and he thought the most likely form in which it could have entered the body was in Rodine rat poison.

Asked if he thought it was possible that Mrs Ricketts administered rat poison to herself after seven o'clock on the morning of her death, the witness said he thought it was reasonably possible, but did not think he was in a position to express an opinion. The judge: 'You have not hesitated to express vigorous and, I can almost say, dogmatic opinions on the strength of what you have seen and heard. Do you feel unable to express an opinion on whether or not it was possible for this woman to have administered rat poison to herself after seven o'clock in the morning?' – 'I do not think it impossible.'

Mr Nahum asked the witness if he was ruling out the possibility of the poison having been ingested by Mrs Ricketts in the early part of the night before she died. Professor Webster replied that he could rule out the possibility of accidental ingestion. The judge: 'Is the suggestion that she liked it so much that, after seven o'clock in the morning, she helped herself to more?' There was no reply.

The Attorney-General: 'Mr Nahum has suggested that one cause of death might have been from the contents of beer bottles from a brewery where rat poison was being used.'

Professor Webster: 'There are many rats in breweries!'

'She might also have been struck by lightning,' retorted the Attorney-General.

Mrs Merrifield, who denied poisoning Mrs Ricketts, told the court that the old lady had been ill on several occasions during the last week of her life. On the night of 13 April she heard Mrs Ricketts getting out of bed and helped her back again. 'She seemed a bit quieter, but when next I heard her up again she was on the floor in the hall,' continued Mrs Merrifield. 'I picked her up and got her into bed. She said she was thankful to me and my husband for what we had done for her. Those were the last words she spoke, at 3.15 am.' She added that Mrs Ricketts apparently lost her speech, but she put out her tongue, indicating that she was thirsty. 'I gave her a sip from an egg-cup of brandy or rum which she had prepared herself the night before. I stayed with her until 8.30 am.'

Mrs Merrifield was asked by the Attorney-General if she knew that a striking sign of phosphorus poison was a great thirst, and she agreed that she had heard that, adding, 'But she suffered from great thirst from the time of us going there. She was always on the thirst for her brandy and the drink.' As Mrs Ricketts was by then desperately ill, she went for a doctor and tried three times before she was successful. She was questioned by the Attorney-General about why she did not go for a doctor earlier, at 3.15 am, and replied: 'Well, it was not a nice time of the morning to go out on the streets and call a doctor.' The judge: 'Are you saying you did not go for a doctor because it was not a nice time to be out on the streets?' – 'That's right, your lordship.'

Questioned about Mrs Ricketts's will, Mrs Merrifield said it was not true that she had wanted the bungalow from the day she moved in. She had never wanted it but Mrs Ricketts was determined that they should have it.

Asked if she thought that her husband was getting too friendly with the old lady, she replied: 'Well, everybody has their suspicions. She was very fond of him. I found Mrs Ricketts a very immoral woman, but I realized she was a human being and had had no husband for eight or ten years.'

The Attorney-General: 'But Mrs Ricketts was in her eightieth year?' – 'Yes.'

'If you had got the bungalow in your own hands you would not have been dependent upon your husband?' – 'I never loved anyone for what I could get out of them.'

'You were afraid that Mr Merrifield might so please the old

lady that she might alter her will and you would be left out altogether?' – 'No, not at all.'

Mrs Merrifield agreed that she knew that bran was found in the stomach at the post mortem, but said that she did not know what bran was. Asked by the Attorney-General if there was anything in the house which could have produced the bran, she replied: 'There was brown bread.'

'Why mention brown bread if you don't know what bran is?' asked the Attorney-General. 'How did you know you ought to refer to brown bread?'

'Because she liked brown bread and I got two loaves in.'

She denied having 'invented' the brown loaves. She also denied having been to Manchester, having bought Rodine or having told anyone that Mrs Ricketts had died before the death took place. The people who had made those statements were 'just jealous of her because they were all up to their necks in mortgages'.

Alfred Merrifield also denied having anything to do with Mrs Ricketts's death. The old lady, he said, had thanked him for being good and kind to her and had told him he would have a home 'for the longest day he lived'. Mrs Ricketts had spoken to him about changing her will and he thought she meant to make him sole legatee because of the way he had looked after her. He did not tell his wife about this talk.

Merrifield declared that when he and his wife took the job with Mrs Ricketts he found the old lady 'very small and very feeble'.

'She had had a stroke in the right arm and leg,' he said, 'and had both arms wrapped up in cotton wool and bandages. I thought she was a very heavy drinker for an old lady.'

On the day of Mrs Ricketts's death he had got up at about 9.0 am and seen that she was dying. She mumbled to him that she was not well. The Attorney-General: 'If, as you say, you were fond of the old lady, would it not have been a good thing to get up during the night and see how she was getting on?' Merrifield: 'I am a cripple. It is definite I should have my rest. There was a capable lady there, my wife, to attend to her.'

'I am bound to suggest to you that Mrs Ricketts died by poisoning of phosphorus and you were concerned in that death.' – 'Definitely not. Why should I poison the old lady for a few bricks and mortar?'

Questioned about allegations that he had bought a tin of Rodine in a Manchester chemist's shop, Merrifield replied that he had not been to Manchester for five years and had not been outside Blackpool for twelve months because he had ulcers on his legs. Banging his fist on the witness-box, he shouted: 'It's perjured evidence, all cooked up by Scotland Yard men.'

When Mr Nahum said it had been suggested that there had been some impropriety with Mrs Ricketts, Merrifield replied: 'A more infamous statement has never been made in a court of justice. It is definitely not true. Fancy, an old woman of eighty paralysed down one side. It's outrageous. Look at my wife, a young woman. Fancy me getting into bed with an old woman of eighty.'

As Mr Nahum began his final address to the jury, Merrifield burst into tears, crying: 'I cannot stick this. It is not fair. Let me go down until they have finished this.' The court adjourned to allow him time to recover.

Mr Nahum said that the prosecution had failed to supply sufficient proof that phosphorus was introduced into the body of Mrs Ricketts, that phosphorus caused her death or that the Merrifields administered the fatal dose. Professor Webster had said that Mrs Ricketts died from natural causes – from liver necrosis due to diet insufficiency in a woman who took alcohol – and if this evidence was accepted, then it could not be murder. Mrs Merrifield's alleged conversations before the old lady's death were nothing more than 'the stupid vapourings of a woman who could not wait to tell everyone that she had been left a lovely little bungalow'. Had she really been contemplating the murder of Mrs Ricketts she would not have been likely to talk about her death before it occurred. As for Mr Merrifield, he was quite guileless, a tragic simpleton incapable of doing what the prosecution had suggested.

Mr Justice Glyn-Jones: 'Supposing the jury find that one or other of these accused administered Rodine rat poison to Mrs Ricketts, intending to kill her, and that she died not of the rat poison but of natural causes – what is the proper verdict?' Mr Nahum: 'It must be attempted murder.'

Summing up for the prosecution, the Attorney-General told

the jury that the possibilities of accident or suicide could be ruled right out of the picture. 'I am bound to submit that there is a most terrible case against these two people,' he said. 'I told you in opening that there was only one thing missing and that was evidence of administration of the poison. However unpalatable it may be, you cannot avoid the conclusion that there is the strongest evidence of how and when this poison was administered . . . there is of course, the possibility that a dying rat came through the window and that phosphorus was deposited that way. How it got into Mrs Ricketts' throat would be a further matter for speculation.' It was fantastic, he said, to suggest that the old lady got up in the middle of the night and took rat poison, disposing of the container in a way in which it could not later be discovered.

Summing up, the judge described Alfred Merrifield as 'somewhat foolish', and told the jury: 'You may have formed the opinion that Mrs Merrifield was a rather vulgar and stupid woman with a dirty mind. I do her no injustice in telling you that, but the fact that she is vulgar and stupid is no ground to convict her of murder.' Neither did it matter that Mrs Ricketts had made a will in favour of the Merrifields. The point to be considered was whether the fact that the will had been made in their favour operated on the Merrifields' minds subsequently.

After a retirement of nearly six hours, the jury found Mrs Merrifield guilty of murder but said that they were unable to agree on Mr Merrifield. Sentencing her to death, Mr Justice Glyn-Jones told Mrs Merrifield that she had been convicted upon plain evidence of 'a wicked and cruel murder'. Her appeal against conviction, during a hearing which lasted three days, was dismissed on 3 September 1953, and she was hanged at Strangeways Jail on 18 September.

There was a great deal of legal argument about whether or not Alfred Merrifield should be retried, but conjecture was ended when, on the personal decision of Sir Lionel Heald, a *nolle prosequi* was entered in the case. This had the effect of staying further proceedings against Merrifield, although it did not rank as an acquittal and it was still legally within the power of the Crown to institute fresh proceedings.

Those proceedings were never taken. When he was released

from prison he was given the key to the bungalow in which Mrs Ricketts died. He lived there for some time while lawyers argued about the will which had made him and his wife the sole beneficiaries. It was three years before a settlement was announced and he was then granted one-sixth of the £2,000 estate, the rest going to Mrs Ricketts's two daughters.

He was paid £500 for the use of his effigy (since removed) in the Chamber of Horrors at Madame Tussaud's and, after trying unsuccessfully to find lodgings – it is said that seventy-four landladies refused to accommodate him – bought a caravan in Blackpool. There he lived alone until he died at the age of eighty in June 1962, taking with him to the grave the secrets of what really happened on that night in April 1953.

There were four men in the life of Mary Elizabeth Wilson – and each one died from phosphorus poisoning. Yet if this plain, bespectacled, dumpy little ginger-haired woman had not been so incredibly sure of herself, it is doubtful if – at the age of sixty-six – she would have stood her trial for murder.

She was first married when she was twenty to John Knowles, twelve years her senior, the son of the house in which she worked as a domestic servant. They lived together for forty-three years and during much of that period their home was shared by John George Russell, a lodger who was also believed to be Mary Knowles's lover.

In August 1955 Knowles died at the age of seventy-five, at the house in which he lived with his wife and Russell in Collingwood Street, Hebburn-on-Tyne, County Durham. Dr F. Hall certified Knowles's death as being from chronic bronchitis and heart failure. He was a retired chimney sweep and all he left his wife was £27. She continued to live in the house with John Russell and there was a good deal of sympathy for her when he, too, died only five months later, the cause of death being certified by Dr J. Skinner as thrombosis, hardening of the arteries and acute bronchitis. Mary Elizabeth thought she was doing a little better that time because he left her £70 in his will, but by the time the debts were paid there was only £6 left.

No one had any reason to doubt that the deaths of these two elderly men were other than natural.

In the summer of 1956 the widow, then aged sixty-four, was introduced to a retired estate agent, Oliver James Leonard, who at the time was lodging with Mrs Mary Alice Connelly and her husband at Albert Road, Jarrow. Soon after this meeting Mrs Knowles asked Mrs Connelly: 'Has that old bugger got any money?' Mrs Connelly said she thought he had a little and Mrs Knowles immediately said she would visit 'the poor old soul'.

She called twice to see Leonard, a hale and hearty old man of seventy-five, and within a few days Leonard had packed his bags and gone to lodge with Mrs Knowles at Collingwood Street. Three days later, however, she called at the Connellys' house and said: 'Come and get that old man out of my house. He will not sign any money over to me until he puts the ring on my finger, so get the old bugger out.' After twenty-four hours' reflection, however, she apparently decided that it might be easier to get hold of his money if he did put the ring on her finger, and the following day returned to tell Mrs Connelly: 'You have no need to bother taking him back. We have made it up and have decided to get married.'

So Mary Elizabeth Knowles became Mrs Leonard at Jarrow Register Office on 20 September 1956. She said later that shortly after they were married Leonard 'took a nasty cold and got doddery on his legs'. On 1 October he called at the surgery of Dr J. H. Laydon in St John's Terrace, Jarrow, and was given some cough mixture. The doctor thought him a healthy man for his age although he was suffering from some bronchitis and breathlessness.

On 3 October 1956 – just thirteen days after the wedding – Mr William Shervington and his sister, Mary Jane, neighbours in Collingwood Street, were awakened in the early hours by Mrs Leonard knocking on their door. When they went into the Leonards' house they found the old man lying on the floor. He was breathing heavily, in obvious pain, and could not speak. Miss Shervington made some tea and offered him a cup, but he knocked it from her hand and she told Mrs Leonard, 'I think he's dying.' 'I think so, too,' replied Mrs Leonard. 'I called you because you'll be handy if he does.'

He did die – without the benefit of medical attention. Later that day his widow called at Dr Laydon's surgery and reported his death. The doctor issued a certificate stating the cause of death to be myocardiao degeneration and nephritis (kidney disease). Mary Elizabeth Leonard collected £50, the total estate of her late lamented second husband – and immediately set about looking for a replacement.

She found Ernest George Lawrence Wilson, a seventy-five-year-old retired engineer living in a council bungalow in Rectory road, Windy Nook, Felling-on-Tyne, County Durham. She wrote to him upon hearing that he was looking for a housekeeper, but he replied to say that he was actually hoping to find a wife. The poor old chap was virtually signing his own death warrant when, in a pathetic effort to induce the widow to marry him and care for him, he told her that he had £100 invested in the local Co-operative Society and a paid-up insurance policy worth £150. Mary Elizabeth needed no further persuasion and on 28 October 1957, again at Jarrow Register Office, she became Mrs Wilson – a little more than a year after the death of her second husband and only twenty-six months following the death of her first.

After the ceremony the couple held a jolly wedding party at the Alnwick Castle Hotel, Jarrow, where Wilson played the piano to entertain their guests. Somebody remarked that there was going to be a lot of sandwiches and cakes left over, to which the bride gaily retorted, 'Just keep them for the funeral!' By way of an afterthought, she added, 'But I might give this one a week's extension.'

Although everybody laughed, there were some who thought uncomfortably of Oliver Leonard . . . and John Russell . . . and John Knowles . . .

The Wilsons returned to Windy Nook and apparently settled down normally to their new married life. Exactly two weeks after the wedding Dr W. P. Wallace, of Wreckenton, Gateshead, who had been Wilson's doctor for many years, was called to the bungalow by Mrs Wilson. She told him that her husband had been ill during the night after eating some liver. The old man, however, was quite cheerful and told the doctor that he could not understand what all the fuss was about. Dr Wallace examined him and decided that he was suffering from myocardiao degeneration of the heart – a condition he had had for many years.

Next morning, 12 November 1957, Dr Wallace received an urgent telephone call to say that Wilson was very ill and he went at once to the bungalow at Windy Nook. Wilson was dead. Dr Wallace thought that death had occurred some three or four hours previously. He gave a certificate which recorded the cause of death as cardio-muscular failure due to myocardiao degeneration.

Even at this stage Mrs Wilson might have got away with her crimes had she not indulged in some extraordinary behaviour which was bound to draw attention to the circumstances of the death and told some lies so blatant that they were immediately obvious as falsehoods.

On the evening of 12 November she called on Mrs Grace Liddell, a widowed acquaintance, of Frobisher street, Hebburn – getting her out of bed to answer the door – and asked if she might stay the night. Mrs Liddell inquired if there was some trouble with Mr Wilson. Mrs Wilson assured her there was no trouble but that her husband was 'badly' and had been seen by a doctor. She stayed overnight with Mrs Liddell and the following morning the two women went together to the Wilsons' home. Mrs Wilson handed the door key to Mrs Liddell, inviting her to go in first and remarking, 'When you get in you'll get a shock.'

Mrs Liddell certainly did get a shock. Wilson's dead body dressed in a white shroud, was laid out on a trestle table. Asked by Mrs Liddell if she had done anything to the old man, Mrs Wilson replied, 'Don't be silly. I have never hurt him.' She then volunteered the information that he had died in hospital and seemed quite unperturbed when her friend pointed out that had that been the case the hospital authorities would either have kept him there or sent him home in a coffin.

Later the same day Mrs Wilson went into the Alnwick Castle Hotel – where her last wedding reception had been held – and told the bar manager, William Walker, that her husband was very ill in the Queen Elizabeth Hospital.

It was not long before the whispers started. Three husbands and a lover dead in just over two years . . . the tasteless cracks about death at the wedding reception . . . the lies . . . the odd behaviour.

In the early hours of the morning of 30 November 1957

three police cars moved quietly into Jarrow cemetery and there, in lashing rain and by the ghostly light of lanterns, a team of policemen began the macabre task of exhuming the bodies of Oliver Leonard and Ernest Wilson. At the Home Office Forensic Science Laboratory at Gosforth it was found that both bodies contained elemental phosphorus and bran – two ingredients of rat and beetle poison.

Detective Chief Inspector Alexander Mitchell told Mrs Wilson that he wanted her to go with him to Jarrow Police Station. 'I know what it will be about,' replied the widow. 'I will come with you and help you all I can. I have nothing to hide.' In a written statement she said: 'If Mr Leonard or Mr Wilson had been poisoned it is through something they both must have eaten outside. Whatever they had to eat while I was married to them was cooked by me. The only thing I can think regarding Mr Wilson is he bought some liver one day and blamed this for making him feel ill. He had cooked it himself, but everything else he had to eat was cooked by me.'

On 11 December 1957 Mary Elizabeth Wilson was accused of murdering Leonard and Wilson. She stood trial on these charges at Leeds Assizes in March 1958 before Mr Justice Hinchcliffe and a jury of nine men and three women. Mr Geoffrey Veale QC appeared for the prosecution and Mrs Wilson was defended by Miss Rose Heilbron QC.

According to Mr Veale, the case was a simple one of 'a wicked woman who married in succession two men and then deliberately poisoned them in order to get the paltry benefits she hoped she might obtain.' To Miss Heilbron, however, the widow was a woman 'who had gone through a heavy ordeal and a terrible agony' and was not the diabolical poisoner she was said to be. But the burden of proof, one way or the other, lay largely with the 'laboratory detectives', and, as so often happens in such cases, they failed to agree on many points. A great part of the six-day trial was taken up with the evidence and cross-examination of the experts.

Pathologist Dr William Stewart, who was present when the two bodies were exhumed and who performed the post-mortem examinations, said that in his opinion the deaths were not due to the causes given on the certificates but appeared to be cases of acute phosphorus poisoning. Cross-examined by Miss Heilbron, he said that these were the first cases of phosphorus poisoning on which he had conducted post mortems. When Dr Ian Barclay, of the Forensic Science Laboratory, Gosforth, said that he had found yellow phosphorus in both bodies, Miss Heilbron asked him: 'Have you heard of many cases where phosphorus has been found in a body after thirteen months?' Dr Barclay replied: 'I know of no other case longer than six months.'

'Is it not therefore surprising to find phosphorus in a body so long after?' – 'I don't think so. There must always be a first time. Yellow phosphorus can be protected by the fatty material and its free state preserved.'

Questioned about the amount of elemental phosphorus constituting a fatal dose, Dr Barclay said that a fair amount had to be taken to make sure that a small proportion got to work; 1 grain was equivalent to 64.5 milligrams, so a fatal dose of $1\frac{1}{2}$ grains was about 100 milligrams.

Dr Alan Currie, Scientific Officer, Home Office Laboratory, Harrogate, said that Dr Barclay sent him some specimens for analysis to see if he could find in them any drug or poison other than phosphorus. He found none. For his own interest he also tested for elemental phosphorus and obtained positive results. Asked by Miss Heilbron if he had heard of elemental phosphorus being used in pills, Dr Currie said he had never come across it, but added, 'There are many strange things used in pills.' Miss Heilbron then handed him a bottle of pills, used as an aphrodisiac, and asked him to smell them. The witness crushed one pill with a coin and sniffed the powder. 'Yes,' he said, 'there is a little phosphorus there, or at least the smell of it.'

Dr David Price, another pathologist, said that phosphorus could get through the skin or small wounds if a person was exposed to it. To produce death it would be necessary to ingest about a teaspoonful, but the amount of phosphorus found in a body after death was not a guide to the amount taken. It was merely a residue left after death had occurred. Mr Justice Hinchcliffe: 'In your opinion, what were the causes of these deaths?' 'I think both men died in the first stage of phosphorus poisoning,' replied Dr Price.

In her opening speech for the defence, Miss Heilbron referred to the aphrodisiac pills and commented, 'What more natural than that these old men, finding a wife in the evening of their lives, should purchase these pills for the purpose for which they are apparently known.'

The first defence witness, Mr Angus McIntosh, manager of Thomas Harley Ltd, of Perth, manufacturers of Rodine rat poison, told the court that he had examined some of these pills, which were used to increase sexual desire and for the treatment of sexual debility. Each pill contained one-hundredth of a grain of elemental phosphorus and there were fifty pills in a bottle. Mr Veale: 'So to get a fatal dose you would have to take about one hundred and fifty pills – three whole bottles?' – 'That's right.'

Dr Francis Camps, Home Office pathologist, who was called as a defence witness, said that the findings of the cause of death were pathologically contradictory and he would be very chary of diagnosing first-stage phosphorus poisoning. If he was asked to suggest a cause of death in these cases he would say that Wilson had died from heart failure and Leonard from cerebral thrombosis. These were merely suggestions and if he was asked to put a cause of death he would say that the cause was unascertainable.

Mr Veale questioned Dr Camps about symptoms and said, 'In Leonard's case we have a pallor, pain, restlessness and mental change.'

'That is only a picture of anyone dying,' replied Dr Camps.

'You said Wilson died of heart failure, that something stopped his heart. Might it have been phosphorus poisoning?' – 'It could have been. The only thing that worries me is that there are too many things missing.'

The witness said that he had been concerned in a number of phosphorus poisoning cases and described what he called first- and second-stage cases. In first-stage cases death usually occurred between six and ten hours after sickness, pain, intense thirst and prostration. In second-stage cases death took longer, causing changes in the liver condition. He thought that if Leonard and Wilson had died of phosphorus poisoning they were second-stage cases because of the changes that had taken place in the livers.

Dr Camps said that in a previous case tests had been made with beer, cider, bread, jam, tea and spirits to see how far it was possible to disguise the taste of rat poison. It was found that blackcurrant jam effectively masked the taste, but in that case he would have expected to find evidence of the jam. 'To take rat poison raw the person would have to be blind and have no sense of taste or smell because as soon as you open the tin there is a strong odour,' he commented. Mr Veale then handed a bottle to Dr Camps and asked him what he thought it contained. The witness replied that it smelt like cough mixture. Dr Price was recalled to the witness box to say that the bottle in fact contained cough mixture to which he had added a good teaspoonful of Rodine.

Miss Heilbron told the jury that, on the advice of her counsel, Mrs Wilson was not going into the witness box.

'She has given a very full and frank statement to the police. She has said the deaths are a mystery and she certainly cannot assist you on the scientific side. Don't hold it against her – because she has accepted my advice.'

The judge: 'The jury do not want to know what advice you gave the prisoner. You know you should not have said it.' Miss Heilbron apologized.

In his summing-up Mr Justice Hinchcliffe made reference to Mrs Wilson's failure to give evidence on oath. 'You are without explanation upon many important matters,' he said. 'Not only on what were the symptoms of her two husbands, but as to the length and detail of their illnesses, the reason why a doctor was not called in, her odd behaviour on 12 November and her queer and untrue account that Wilson was ill when he was already dead.'

The jury was out for one hour and twenty-five minutes before finding Mrs Wilson guilty of both murders. Under the Homicide Act of 1957, murder by poisoning did not carry the death penalty, but the Act provided that a person convicted of more than one murder was guilty of a capital offence and liable to sentence of death. The thrice-widowed poisoner was accordingly sentenced to death and the date of her execution was fixed for 4 June 1958, but a last-minute reprieve saved her from the gallows and the sentence was commuted to life imprisonment.

Five days after she went to prison an inquest was held on her first husband, John Knowles, and her lodger and lover, John Russell, whose bodies had been exhumed while she was awaiting trial. Dr William Stewart, who gave evidence at the trial on his post mortem findings in the cases of Leonard and Wilson, also examined the bodies of Knowles and Russell and again formed the opinion that their deaths had been due to phosphorus poisoning. Detective Chief Inspector Mitchell said that he could not produce any evidence to show how the phosphorus came to be in the bodies and the Jarrow coroner, Mr Alan Henderson, returned an open verdict in each case.

The widow's life sentence was four-and-a-half years. She died in Holloway Prison on 5 December 1962, at the age of seventy.

6

Men who poisoned

Although some of the most notorious poisoners of the last century have been women, a number of men, too, have chosen this way of disposing of their victims. Not the least prominent was the dandyish Jean Pierre Vacquier, a Frenchman. He poisoned Alfred Jones, the landlord of the Blue Anchor Hotel at Byfleet, Surrey, by lacing his morning dose of health salts with strychnine. The trial caused something of a sensation because it revealed a love affair between Vacquier and the landlord's wife and was punctuated throughout by dramatic outbursts and gestures from the dock. Vacquier, who spoke no English and had to have an interpreter, was found guilty and hanged at Wandsworth in August 1924.

Another male poisoner – who almost successfully concealed homicide – was Dr Robert George Clements, an Irishman and one time Assistant Medical Officer of Health at Blackburn, Lancashire. He killed himself when he realized that he was likely to be arrested for murdering his fourth wife, Amy, in 1947. A second post mortem on Mrs Clements – the first involved an error of judgement which resulted in the suicide of the doctor concerned – showed that she had died from morphine poisoning and not from leukaemia, as her husband asserted. There was a strong suspicion that he had also murdered his first, second and third wives, in each case to inherit their money.

Vacquier used strychnine and Clements chose morphine, but there are many, many ways of killing by poisoning and the choice of substance is usually governed by its availability to the murderer. Among the gaseous and liquid poisons, wood alcohol, lysol and prussic acid have all been used, while phosphorus, arsenic and spirits of salts might be described as the most popular in the group of metallic and inorganic poisons.

As any reader of detective stories knows, fungus poisons and snake venoms can cause death, but among these vegetable and animal poisons morphine and strychnine are the most commonly used in real life. Additionally there are the organic poisons, which include aspirin, phenobarbitone and hypnotics of the barbituric acid group, so often mentioned in cases of suicide.

From the police point of view the major hurdle to be overcome in cases of murder by poison is to know, quite simply, that it has taken place. Where violent death occurs – shooting, strangling, battering – detectives are usually on the scene shortly after the discovery of the body, but murder by poison can easily appear to be a natural death and unless the doctor who is called has any reason to be suspicious the police may know nothing about it until after the destruction of clues which could help them to differentiate between accident, suicide or murder. Some poisons leave their own clues, like the contraction of the pupils of the eyes in cases of morphine, opium and nicotine poisoning and dilation of the pupils where belladonna or cocaine have been administered. Strychnine causes convulsions and the drawing up of the corners of the mouth so that the dead person's face appears to wear a fixed grin. The vomit and excrement of a sick person can give clear indications to a doctor of some other poisons if he already has suspicions about the cause of the illness.

Often, however, the first indication to the police that a 'natural' death may be unnatural comes from the whispers of suspicious relatives or an anonymous letter of the 'Are you aware . . . ?' type. In the interests of justice it is fortunate that most poisons can be detected after death, in some cases even after many years, so that no poisoner can ever feel safe. Strychnine and morphine remain for several years and arsenic can be discovered in a skeleton centuries after death.

In the case of Beryl Waite, however, an exhumation was not necessary. She had been ill for months and when she died, on 8 September 1969, one of the family doctors issued a death certificate giving the cause of death as acute gastro-enteritis with allergic polyneuropathy (extensive nerve damage) as a contributory factor.

Then he began to think back – and the things he remembered worried him. He realized that one possible cause of both conditions affecting his patient was arsenic poisoning and he decided, as a precautionary measure, to inform the coroner. On the day before the day her funeral should have taken place, a post-mortem examination was carried out on the body of forty-five-year-old Beryl Waite, wife of William Charles Waite, personal chauffeur to Lord Leigh, of Stoneleigh Abbey, Warwickshire. The doctor's suspicions proved to be well founded. She had died of a massive dose of arsenic, the final dose in a number administered over a period of more than a year. The funeral was stopped and William Waite, a tall, good-looking man four years younger than his wife, was closely questioned. He said that he had no idea how arsenic could have entered his wife's body, but suggested that she might have taken her own life. It was a story from which he never deviated throughout his subsequent trial for her murder, but the story uncovered by the police team led by Detective Superintendent Brian Scarth, head of Warwick CID, was a very different one.

The story really started in 1949 when Waite, a soldier in the Royal Tank Regiment, met pretty Beryl Walden. They married in 1952 after a conventional courtship and in the same year Waite, whose father had been batman to Lord Leigh during the war, started work at Stoneleigh Abbey. The couple occupied a pleasant flat on the estate, two children were born – Julie first and William Robin two years later – and they settled down to happy family life. Among his other duties Waite accompanied Lord Leigh on hunting and shooting expeditions to Scotland and different parts of England. His wife stayed at home, looking after the children and working as a domestic help at Stoneleigh Abbey three days a week.

Life moved uneventfully for the Waites for more than fourteen years. Then, in the summer of 1966, a girl called Judith Regan left the Roman Catholic secondary school in Warwick and got her first job – as a typist in the estate office at Stoneleigh Abbey. She was seventeen, a petite, dark, attractive girl with a quiet manner, a girl who until then had led a sheltered life, having no serious boyfriends and preferring to spend her spare time sewing and reading. William Waite, who was frequently in the estate office, noticed the girl, but made no effort to get to know her better until a 1967 Christmas party given at the home of Jack Delany, head groom at Lord Leigh's stables. Waite and Miss Regan danced together several times and towards the end of the party, when somebody turned out the lights, he kissed her. A few days later Waite invited Judith then just nineteen, to a New Year's party at his own home. She was flattered and thrilled. Again they kissed during a 'lights out' dance.

Whether William Waite decided that this was a dangerous attraction which must be resisted, or whether the party kisses were so unimportant to him that he forgot about the girl, is something no one is ever likely to know. Certainly he made no effort to contact her again for some weeks. So far as Judith Regan was concerned, the party was over. Then, towards the end of January, Waite walked into her office and asked her if she would go out with him that night. They spent the evening drinking in a village pub, then kissed and cuddled in his red Volkswagen in a country lane. Two weeks later the invitation was repeated and this time they had sexual intercourse in the back of the car. That was the beginning of a passionate undercover affair which was to increase in its intensity throughout 1968 and into the spring and summer of 1969. They spent at least one evening a week together, then came occasional nights at hotels, and whenever there was an opportunity they enjoyed a weekend at a motel or hotel, registering as Mr and Mrs White.

About a year after their first outing they began to discuss the possibility of divorce for Waite and there was vague talk of marriage and a honeymoon in Majorca. Waite promised Miss Regan that he would tell his wife the truth and persuade her to divorce him, but he made no move towards this end and in fact when his wife asked him if there was anything between him and the girl he denied having any interest in Miss Regan.

His children, too, were becoming suspicious. William found a handkerchief smelling of Miss Regan's perfume in the car, and Julie, then fourteen, who knew that her mother took the pill, discovered a packet of contraceptives while she was cleaning the car. Waite seems to have been worried because he was unable to make love to his wife – that at least is what he told Dr Harold Parker, the family doctor, in September 1968.

He consulted the doctor because, he said, he was finding it extremely difficult to have sexual intercourse with his wife. Dr Parker asked if there was any reason for this and Waite replied: 'If it is a question of any other woman, there is certainly no one else involved.' Waite was given a preparation and later returned to the surgery for another bottle, saying that he was much better.

While he was in Scotland with Lord Leigh in the autumn of 1968 Waite wrote loving letters to his wife, in which he made reference to his inability to have intercourse with her. In the first letter, which began 'My own darling,' he wrote: 'I did not know how to leave you on Sunday, darling. I do so hate being away from you and the children. You all mean all the world to me. Pet, I still love you with all my heart, strange as this may seem to you. I just cannot explain it and I am trying so hard to think why this should be.' The letter was signed, 'Your dear loving husband Bill.' The second letter read: 'I am praying this will work out all right in the end. There must be something wrong with me. Leave the worry to me. Look after yourself. . . . God bless you and keep you safe always.'

Pressures were beginning to build up and at one point Waite and Judith Regan agreed to break off their association. The break was short-lived because within three days Waite was back in the estate office, telling Judith he couldn't live without her.

There is no evidence that Waite was ever less than affectionate towards his wife and it is impossible to speculate on why he decided that murder, rather than divorce, was the answer to his problem. But death was his decision and some time early in 1968 he began to introduce into her food and drink small doses of Paris Green, a pesticide which contains arsenic. On an estate such as Stoneleigh Abbey there are naturally stocks of such materials, so he had no need to arouse suspicion by buying arsenical weed-killer or other poisonous substances. Beryl Waite, normally a healthy, energetic woman, began to grow thin and listless, lost her appetite and could not sleep. In July 1968 she consulted Dr Parker, who prescribed some tablets. She seemed to get a little better, but he continued to see her at monthly intervals until January

1969, when she had a severe attack of vomiting. Then she complained of swelling ankles and numbness in her hands and legs. Dr Parker was puzzled by her illness and arranged for her to be admitted to Warnefort Hospital, Leamington Spa, for observation. Her disorder was diagnosed as acute polyneuritis, believed to be due to a virus or an allergy, and during her stay in hospital her health improved a great deal.

She returned home in April, after a month in hospital, and seemed to be much better, but soon her old troubles returned and she became a semi-invalid. Throughout her illness her husband showed the greatest solicitude, carrying her from one room to another when she lost the use of her legs. Judith Regan was a frequent visitor to the flat, helping with the housework and shopping and sometimes cooking meals for Waite and the two children. Waite and the girl continued to enjoy their weekly outings, usually on Saturdays, when Waite would take drinks and glasses and they would make love in the back of the car, the Volkswagen having by this time been exchanged for a silver-grey Cortina.

On Saturday, 6 September they met as usual and spent about four hours together. Waite drove alone to Hampshire the following day and on his return found that his wife was seriously ill. He telephoned for the doctor and Beryl Waite was seen by Dr John Harger, one of Dr Parker's partners. Waite told him that his wife had gastro-enteritis. Dr Harger gave her an injection and left a sleeping capsule, saying that Dr Parker would call the next day. Waite gave the capsule to his wife in front of her sister, Mrs Georgina Jones, of Leamington Spa, who had been called because Mrs Waite was so ill. This capsule put Beryl Waite into a sleep from which she never awoke, her husband having emptied it and refilled it with arsenic. She died in the early hours of 8 September, weighing only six-and-a-half stone. Dr Harger issued the death certificate, but later that day had second thoughts and after talking the matter over with Dr Parker, contacted the Warwickshire coroner, Dr H. Tibbitts.

Pathologist Dr Derek Barrowcliff examined her body and found that it contained a thousand times as much arsenic as that of a normal person. He concluded that a dose of arsenic had been administered on the Friday before her death, another dose on the Saturday, a massive dose on Sunday morning and a final dose about six hours before her death. He thought she had probably taken a much larger quantity than was actually found, because arsenic passes quickly through the body, and that the poison had been taken from November 1968, or possibly before that time.

Tests he made on segments of her hair pointed to an almost continuous arsenic administration over a long period. One segment was free of arsenic and this represented the period when Mrs Waite was in hospital. Dr Barrowcliff made an experiment which he later described, at the trial, as 'not very scientific, but successful'. Contamination of hair by arsenic in sweat sometimes affects the results of hair arsenic analysis, but Dr Barrowcliff was able to prove that this could not have happened in the case of Mrs Waite. She was always a meticulously neat and well-groomed woman and even three days before her death, although desperately ill, she had sprayed her hair with a lacquer-based fixative in order to keep it in its usual tidy fashion. Dr Barrowcliff sprayed a piece of blotting paper with the lacquer and when it had dried he wrote on it with his fountain-pen. The lacquer stopped the water-soluble ink soaking through to the other side as it would normally do, proving that perspiration could not have penetrated the lacquered hair to leave a deposit of arsenic.

As soon as his wife's body had been removed by the undertakers, Waite destroyed the bedclothes from her bed and cleaned or burned other articles connected with her illness. He overlooked two things, however – a packet of Paris Green in the eaves of the roof of the estate garage where he worked, and in a cupboard at his home an empty dispenser which had contained anti-travel-sickness pills and which, on analysis, also revealed traces of Paris Green.

When Waite was first seen by detectives he made no mention of his association with Judith Regan, but later admitted that he was having a love affair and said that he would have married Judith if he had been free. In reply to a suggestion that he had a motive for murdering his wife, he said: 'I did not kill her, if that's what you mean. I couldn't do that.' Six days after his wife's death Waite attempted to kill himself by swallowing a quantity of aspirin, but was taken to hospital and recovered.

At the time of this suicide attempt he was staying with his parents at Home Farm, Stoneleigh Abbey, and he left a note, addressed to 'Dearest Mum and Dad', in which he wrote: 'I didn't do it, but I can't stand everybody being questioned. So please forgive me for doing this to you all. I could not stop loving Judith. We did try so hard.'

He was arrested and charged with murder. When he stood in the dock at Birmingham Assizes in February 1970, the prosecuting counsel, Mr Michael Davies QC, said Waite's motive was 'as old as the hills'. He was a married man who had fallen for a young girl whom he wanted to marry, but his wife would not give him a divorce, so she had to be removed. He was a man of previous excellent character and no one who knew him would have thought him likely to commit a criminal offence, let alone murder, but from January 1968 until his wife's death he had been carrying on a secret association with Judith Regan, regularly having sexual intercourse with her. Waite had carried on two parallel lives, living one with his wife and the other with Miss Regan. Referring to the events of the last weekend in Mrs Waite's life, Mr Davies said it was true that Waite himself had called for the doctor. 'You must give him credit for that,' he said, 'but you may feel he was confident that he had fooled the doctors, as indeed he had up to the time of his wife's death.'

Judith Regan, who lived with her parents, Mr and Mrs James Regan, at St Michael's Road, Warwick, was called as a prosecution witness and told how she kept a notebook with dates of her meetings with William Waite. They went out together sixty times between January 1968 and April 1969, and after that made car trips about once a week. They had also stayed together as man and wife on three occasions.

Mrs Waite had once asked her if there was anything between Mr Waite and herself and she had replied, 'No', although this was not true. Mrs Waite, she added, had three times threatened to commit suicide, the last time being four days before she died. On that occasion she said that she was losing the use of her hands and legs again. She was very upset and made a reference to sleeping tablets. She had never suggested that she had anything but sleeping pills for a suicide attempt.

Questioned by Mr James Ross QC, defending, Miss Regan

said that Waite was very distressed about his wife's health and did everything he could for her. He had injured his back carrying Mrs Waite up and down the stairs to the flat. 'You wanted to marry this man, didn't you?' asked Mr Ross. 'Did you think there was no hope?' Miss Regan nodded, but when Mr Justice Willis told her that she must answer, she said: 'A little hope, maybe.'

Although Miss Regan said that she was alarmed by Mrs Waite's suicide threats, other witnesses expressed opposing views on whether or not suicide was a probability.

Asked if the discovery of her husband's affair with another woman might have made Beryl Waite contemplate suicide, Mrs Rosalie Waite, the mother of the accused man, replied: 'I think she might have done.' Her daughter-in-law 'just lived for her husband and her children' and must have been very unhappy to learn that he was being unfaithful to her. She would have done almost anything to hold on to her husband.

Dr Harold Parker said that Mrs Waite's behaviour during the time he was treating her was quite inconsistent with her administering poison to herself. 'She fully co-operated in the treatment,' he said. 'I am sure she wanted to get better.' Mrs Waite's sister, Mrs Georgina Jones, told the jury that she had never heard or seen anything which might have suggested that her sister would take her own life. She was not that sort of person. 'She was a very forgiving kind of person,' said Mrs Jones. 'She would have held no malice against anyone.'

Dr Barrowcliff, after giving evidence relating to the arsenic found in the dead woman's body and hair, said that he did not think the poisoning was accidental. 'As far as suicide is concerned,' he added, 'I think it inconceivable that a woman should have used such an unpleasant and distressing and at times painful method. In twenty-five years' experience I have never met a suicide case in which the method remotely resembled chronic arsenic poisoning.'

Waite, when he went into the witness-box, was questioned by both counsel about his attitude towards the two women in his life in the summer of 1969. 'What were your feelings towards Judith?' asked Mr Ross. Waite replied: 'I was getting more and more deeply involved.'

'What were your feelings towards your wife?' – 'They must have been cooling off.'

'What positive steps could you have taken about this affair?' – 'First of all I had to wait till my wife was better. I couldn't leave her as she was.'

'To raise it at any time was going to cause considerable pain?' – 'Yes, I still wasn't sure I could go through with it, but I was going to try. I knew it couldn't come about until Judith was twenty-one.'

Waite said that he found he could not approach his wife sexually while at the same time he was becoming more deeply involved with Miss Regan. 'I still felt a lot for my wife. I didn't want our marriage to end then. I wanted to make the best of what we had got.' He had denied to his wife that there was anything between himself and Judith and at the time he thought she believed him, but afterwards he was not so sure. She had spoken of taking some tablets and several times said she did not want to be a burden to him and the children. He told her not to be so silly.

Mr Davies accused Waite of sending hypocritical love letters to his wife while carrying on his affair with Miss Regan. 'Any woman reading those letters would think she was the only woman in the world to the writer?' he asked: 'Yes,' replied Waite.

'But she was not the only woman in the world to you, was she?' – 'No.'

'There you were, fresh from romping in the back of your car with this young girl, writing these letters to your wife. Weren't those letters a deceit on your wife?' – 'Isn't it possible to love two people?' Asked which woman he had put first at the time, he replied: 'I just don't know.'

There were a number of questions, too, about the poison found in Waite's home and he was asked if he had warned his wife and children that he was storing such a deadly poison in the flat. He said that he had not read the writing on the tin which warned that it was not to be kept in any building housing human beings or animals. 'I suggest you took it home because you knew it was a deadly poison,' said Mr Davies.

'I took it home to poison a wasps' nest,' replied Waite.

Mr Ross told the jury that Waite's love for another woman

had thrown him into an appalling dilemma. Having tasted the 'forbidden fruit', he could not bring himself to confess the affair to his wife, but neither could he bring himself to end it. Miss Regan had come into his life at a time when there was a falling off in the physical side of his marrage and he was morally vulnerable because of his secret affair with this girl. Since his wife's death he had developed an 'obsessional fear' that her suspicions of the clandestine association had driven her to poison herself.

Mr Ross referred to evidence that Mrs Waite had spoken of suicide and asked if it was possible that she made herself ill to 'drive off' Miss Regan by winning sympathy. She might deliberately have left traces of Paris Green in the tablet dispenser.

'Do you think that this silent, introspective, suffering and wronged wife might have wreaked a terrible revenge by leaving these things to be found?' he asked. 'It is no less and no more fantastic than many of the other things which have been suggested to you in this case.'

Speaking of Waite's attempted suicide, Mr Ross said there was an old belief that if a man thought he was going to die he told the truth. 'At a time when he thought this world was nearly rid of him, Waite still protested that he did not murder his wife. He again protested his innocence to a doctor when he regained consciousness in hospital.' There were, Mr Ross maintained, many inexplicable features of the case. A tin contaminated with Paris Green had been thrown into a box in an open cupboard at Waite's home and had remained there until police found it after his wife's death. A guilty man was much more likely to have put it in his pocket and disposed of it later.

Mr Justice Willis, in his summing-up, said the prosecution's case depended largely on circumstantial evidence. 'There is no derogation of evidence to say that it is circumstantial,' he added. 'It would be wrong to say it is merely circumstantial evidence. It is evidence of its own peculiar persuasiveness, if you accept it, but different in quality from direct evidence.' He warned the jury: 'You will not condemn this man because he made a young girl, half his age, his mistress and maintained with her a prolonged clandestine relationship.' Nevertheless it was essential to consider this relationship and such motivating effect as it might have had on Waite's conduct. The jury might think it beyond question that Waite wanted to marry Miss Regan and that his wife therefore presented an obstacle.

On 5 March 1970, after a fifteen-day trial, the all-male jury found William Waite guilty of killing his wife. He was jailed for life.

The Waite case – a man married to a woman several years his senior, a passionate love affair with a much younger woman and the murder of the wife – was in broad outline very much a carbon copy of a murder at Sculthorpe, Norfolk, eleven years previously; but then the trial was held, not in a British court of law, but before a United States Air Force court martial sitting in a former film studio at Denham, Buckinghamshire.

The husband and wife were Master Sergeant Marcus Marymont, aged thirty-seven, and Mary Helen Marymont, a quiet, home-loving, rather religious woman of forty-three. They lived with their three children, thirteen-year-old twins Marcus and Mary, and Harold, aged eight, in married quarters at the US Air Force base at Sculthorpe. They had married in the United States in 1943 and had seemingly been happy together until about 1954 when, according to Marymont, his feelings towards his wife changed after he returned to their home in Hobbsville, North Carolina, following fifteen months in Japan. They moved to a US base in Texas and then, in 1956, Marymont was posted to Britain and brought his wife and family with him.

They settled down amicably and it seemed that a new life was about to begin – until in July that year, Marymont visited a club at Maidenhead, Berkshire, and was introduced to Mrs Cynthia Taylor, aged twenty-three, the attractive manageress of a local garden stores. Separated from her husband, Alan, she lived alone at Sylvester Road, Maidenhead. They were mutually attracted and, because Marymont went to London regularly in connection with his normal duties, were able to meet quite frequently. Sometimes he visited her home, at other times they met in London, and by December 1956 they had become lovers.

Marcus told Cynthia that he was divorced and that his wife

112

and children were living in the United States. He gave her a fur stole costing £15 and later paid £28 for a diamond and sapphire ring which he bought in Maidenhead. He spent Christmas 1957 at her home, and Cynthia was happy in the thought that she would be married to her handsome American airman as soon as she obtained a divorce from her husband. In the meantime, at home in Sculthorpe, Mrs Marymont was very unhappy and confided her worries to some of her friends. She told Mrs Teresa Dunning, wife of a sergeant at the base, that she had written some questions on a piece of paper and given it to Marcus. She could not talk to him about her problems because it made her cry. She was happy on that occasion because her husband, after reading her questions, had put his arm round her and said, 'Of course there is nobody else.'

But the love affair with Cynthia Taylor continued in its intensity and in April 1958 Mrs Marymont discovered a letter that her husband had written to his girl friend but had forgotten to post. It was obvious from the contents that he was deeply in love with Mrs Taylor. Although she was greatly distressed, Mrs Marymont told her husband that she still loved him and would forgive him. He said he would try to break off the association, but in fact continued to see Mrs Taylor at regular intervals.

On 6 June that year Mrs Marymont visited a neighbour, Mrs Miriam Conway, wife of Master Sergeant Francis Conway, and started to cry as soon as she arrived. When Mrs Conway asked what was wrong Mrs Marymont said she had discovered that her husband was going out with another woman. 'She was under terrific emotional pressure,' said Mrs Conway. 'She had found that some money which he had been sent from home had not been used as he had told her. She could not bear to think of him making love to some other woman and then coming home to make love to her.'

Apart from his wife's discovery of his illicit relationship, Marymont was beginning to run into financial difficulties. He had a bank loan of £45, owed £40 on a television set, and had borrowed several sums from colleagues at the base, including £18 to pay a telephone bill. He, too, began to confide in his friends and sought advice from his superior officers. He told Captain William Arrendondo, who worked with him in the same office, that he was proposing to send his wife home to the States. The captain advised against this step, saying: 'If you do that you are going to get more tangled up with this affair here. You won't be able to pay alimony – you can't have your cake and eat it.' At Christmas 1957 Major G. L. Pletcher spoke to Marymont about his personal affairs and the sergeant told him that he could not decide whether to spend Christmas with his family or with Mrs Taylor. Major Pletcher gained the impression that Marymont was so seriously involved with the girl that he was having difficulty in living with his wife. He advised Marymont to tell Mrs Taylor that he was married and to straighten out his family situation before he became further entangled.

In the early part of 1958 Mrs Marymont began to suffer from mysterious stomach upsets. She mentioned this 'gastric trouble' in letters to her mother-in-law, Mrs Gertrude Marymont, of Salinas, California, and told her that the medicine she had been given 'was worse than the illness'. She was evidently very worried about her health because she confided to a friend, Mrs Elizabeth Finke, her belief that if she did not soon return home to America she would 'be making the journey in a box'.

On 8 June 1958 the Marymonts went to lunch with Miss Doris Elms, of Blackfriars Street, King's Lynn, Norfolk. There were nine other guests and they were all served with pork sausages, potatoes, peas and sprouts. Mrs Marymont was very pale and ate hardly anything, explaining to Miss Elms that she had not been feeling too well that week. At 2 pm on 9 June Mrs Marymont was admitted to Sculthorpe base hospital in a state of complete collapse. Her husband told a doctor there that she had been ill throughout the night and that she had suffered similar attacks, though not of such a serious nature, on many occasions in the past year. She was given emergency treatment by three doctors, but died just after 9.45 that evening. Nobody knew the cause of her death but it was assumed to be a natural one.

It was Sergeant Marymont's curious behaviour that first aroused suspicion. Captain Max Buchfuehrer, general medical officer at the hospital, was trying to impress upon Marymont the gravity of his wife's condition when the sergeant interrupted him to talk about his own sexual problems. The doctor was naturally shocked by this reaction and his suspicions were further aroused when, after Mrs Marymont had died, her husband asked him, 'Doctor, what is a toxic liver?' At that time there was not the slightest indication as to the nature of her illness and, after a talk with another doctor, it was decided that a post-mortem examination should be made and organs sent for analysis.

Tests were carried out by Dr Lewis Nickolls, Director of Scotland Yard's Forensic Laboratory. He found evidence of at least three doses of arsenic, one of which had been taken sometime in the twenty-four hours preceding death. Another dose had been taken one or two months earlier and a third one possibly six months before the final fatal dose.

On the day following his wife's death Marymont wrote to his commanding officer and asked for an extension of six months to his overseas tour of duty. He said he was anxious to set up a home for his three children before the end of the school term. On 14 June he went to Maidenhead and told Cynthia Taylor that his wife had died. She asked him, 'In America?' and he replied, 'No, here in England. She came over with me.' It was only then that Mrs Taylor learned that he was not divorced and had, in fact, been living with his wife throughout the whole of his association with her. In spite of this deception, her feelings for him remained the same and it was arranged that they should marry as soon as she was free to do so.

Five weeks after the death of Mary Marymont her husband was arrested on a charge of 'suspicion of involvement' and his children were flown back to the United States. Investigations continued and in December 1958 he stood before the court martial on two charges: premeditated murder of his wife by the administration of arsenic; and wrongfully having sexual intercourse with a woman not his wife – adultery being an offence under American military law.

The court martial was convened in the old film studio – the headquarters of the 7500 United States air base group. The 'judges' – two colonels, four lieutenant-colonels, six majors, two captains and a lieutenant – sat in front of the United

115

States flag. I reported the hearing in a 'courtroom' atmosphere that was a strange contrast to an English court of law – the legal jargon could have been directly extracted from an Erle Stanley Gardner Perry Mason murder trial.

One of the chief witnesses called by prosecuting counsel, Major C. J. Lewis, was the Scotland Yard expert, Dr Nickolls who explained his findings relating to arsenic in the body. The arsenic in the liver, he said, indicated that a lethal dose of between 2 and 3 grains had been taken within twenty-four hours before death. Hair samples from the dead woman showed arsenic towards the roots, indicating that another dose of the poison had been ingested some time before death – a minimum of one month. Further up the hair he had discovered more arsenic, which had probably been taken about six months previously. Dr Nickolls explained that the arsenic had been deposited in the hair and, as it grew, took the arsenic with it. He was not able to determine the form in which the poison was ingested.

Another expert witness was Dr Francis Camps, Home Office pathologist, who was first questioned about his qualifications and asked by Major Lewis how many autopsies he had performed. 'I should say at least sixty thousand,' replied Dr Camps.

The doctor described experiments that he and his colleagues had carried out with arsenic and said that in a chocolate solution the poison was undetectable by taste unless very large quantities were dissolved. There was no taste up to 10 grains. Within twenty minutes of taking arsenic by mouth, however, a burning sensation was experienced in the gullet. Even when the mouth was rinsed after spitting out the poison he and his colleagues had still experienced the burning sensation.

Questioned by Major Lewis, the witness said that he had no way of knowing whether a dose of arsenic was self-administered or not. 'Do you know whether people who take poison to commit suicide are likely to admit it on questioning when seriously ill?' asked Major Lewis. Dr Camps replied, 'I would say that with one exception it is unusual for the people not to say, and that exception is aspirin. People who take poison to get sympathy are usually only too anxious to live.'

Charles Waterson, of Grove Side, King's Lynn, Norfolk, a civilian cleaner at the Sculthorpe Air Base, told the court that while he was sweeping out the chemical laboratory one night in May that year a master sergeant came in and looked at some shelves on which there were bottles of chemicals. This sergeant, who was 'similar to Marymont', made some remark about the quantity of chemicals there and mentioned 'even arsenic'. Waterson replied, 'Yes, you would not have to take a lot of that.' Another cleaner, James Twide, of East Rudham, Norfolk, also on duty that night, identified the master sergeant as Marymont. 'He asked if they didn't keep that stuff locked up and I told him they did not,' said Twide. 'The sergeant said they ought to and he then picked up several bottles and looked at them.'

Further evidence of Marymont's interest in arsenic was given by Mr Bernard Sampson, a pharmacist, of High Street, Maidenhead, who said that he kept arsenic at his shop but was not permitted to sell it without completing a police form stating the purpose for which it was required 'On 23 or 24 May Marymont came into the shop during the afternoon and asked me if we kept arsenic,' said Mr Sampson. 'I said we did but we should want a permit. He said, " Oh, all right " and went out.'

Cross-examined by Captain Neil Casdan, defence counsel, the witness said that Marymont was in the shop for only a few seconds. He agreed that he had later been shown a sheet of photographs and had picked out one. Asked by Major Lewis why he remembered the man who had called at his shop, Mr Sampson replied, 'Because he made such an odd request and he spoke such good English with an American accent.'

Cynthia Taylor, who was often in tears and eventually had to be helped from the court by a nurse, gave evidence lasting seven-and-a-half hours during two days of the hearing. Much of the time was spent in the identification of nearly seventy letters written by her to Marymont and later found in a drawer of his desk at the Sculthorpe base. She said that marriage was first discussed between her and Marymont some time in 1957 and he had promised to marry her when she got her divorce, which she thought would be by the end of 1958.

Although Marymont had pleaded not guilty to both charges,

117

he told the court martial that he wished to testify only on the murder charge. He admitted having sexual relations with Mrs Taylor from Christmas 1956 until May 1958 and had known from the time they first met that she was a married woman. He emphatically denied attempting to administer arsenic to his wife and said that he had never at any time tried to buy arsenic. He had applied for an extension of his overseas tour after his wife's death because he wanted his children to continue their education in Britain. He needed an additional six months so that his mother could come over to help him.

Major Lewis asked the sergeant: 'Are you deeply in love with Mrs Taylor?'

'You mean at the present time?' queried Marymont.

'The present time, the past time, any time . . .'

'During the past two years I would say I was in love with Mrs Taylor, not deeply in love.'

Handing him a letter, Major Lewis asked: 'When you wrote this letter would you say you were deeply in love with her?'

'I have no way of knowing when it was written. I would not say the tone of that letter indicates that I was deeply in love with her.'

When Major Lewis suggested that Mrs Taylor would by that time have been Mrs Marymont if there had been no hitch, Marymont replied: 'No, I knew she was not eligible till September this year.'

'But this very month, December, would have been the month assuming there had been no hitch?' – 'Yes.'

'She was fully expecting to be your wife by now?' – 'Yes, she was not aware of my marital situation.'

Marymont agreed that he had undertaken to adopt Mrs Taylor's son – born in October 1956, three months after their first meeting – on the understanding that they were to be married.

Questioned about leaving his three children at Sculthorpe to visit Mrs Taylor five days after his wife's death, Marymont said that they did not need him. They had shown little sign of emotion when he broke the news of their mother's death.

Mrs Mary Russell, wife of a staff sergeant, gave evidence that Mrs Marymont had said of her husband: 'I will see

118

him dead in hell before I break my family up.'

After a trial lasting ten days the court adjudicators were absent for five-and-a-half hours before they gave their verdict by secret ballot – guilty of the murder of his wife and guilty of having unlawful sexual intercourse with Mrs Taylor. A further secret ballot decided the sentence of hard labour for life, dishonourable discharge from the service and forfeiture of all allowances.

The findings and sentence were automatically subject to three reviews. At the first of these appeals, Mr William Mars-Jones QC and Mr W. M. F. Hudson put the case for Marymont before the Staff Judge Advocate at the USAF Third Air Force Headquarters at Denham. Mr Mars-Jones said that a letter from Marymont's mother should have been produced at the trial. This letter spoke of a friend who had died of cancer and of Marymont's wife having said that she 'would take something' rather than suffer in a similar manner. She might have feared that she was suffering from cancer. It was also possible on the evidence, said Mr Mars-Jones, that Mrs Marymont had taken arsenic either to commit suicide or in an attempt to gain sympathy by making herself ill. It was significant that on each occasion when she was alleged to have ingested arsenic her husband was planning to go away. Each time his departure was delayed by his wife's illness and it was reasonably possible that she had taken the poison in order to keep him at home or to frighten him.

This appeal failed and after a further review the sentence of hard labour for life was confirmed. Marymont was sent to Fort Leavenworth jail in Kansas, USA, and in August 1960, after a new trial, heard his conviction for murder upheld by the US Court of Military Appeals. This court set aside his conviction on the adultery charge. In 1962, four years after his first trial, his life sentence was cut to thirty-five years.

7

The ballistics experts

Guns and bullets have their own stories to tell. To the men trained in the science of ballistics, each weapon is as clearly distinctive as fingerprints. The machine-finished metal surface of the inside of a gun barrel is never absolutely flawless, so when a bullet is fired it becomes imprinted with a pattern of tiny irregularities matching those of the barrel. Similarly recognisable marks may be left by the imprint of the firing pin on the ignition cap and, in automatic pistols, by the ejector on the empty cartridge case. The marks produced by any given gun can be considered unique, so that it is possible for ballistics experts to say without fear of contradiction, '*This* bullet was fired from *this* gun.'

The tracks of the bullet through a body can tell a great deal about the angle from which the shot was fired, while marks on the dead person's clothing provide a good guide to the distance between murderer and victim at the time of the shooting.

One of the biggest mistakes made by the killer of company director Joseph Hayes – shot dead on the doorstep of his home in Longbridge Road, Barking, Essex, on July 23 1964 – was to use a weapon so unusual that it gave an immediate clue to his identity. Mr Hayes, aged sixty-seven, was the managing director of two ship-repairing companies and his sixty-six-year-old wife, Mrs Elsie May Hayes, was the company secretary. It was their normal practice on Thursdays to draw cash from the bank for the payment of staff wages the following day, and on the evening of Thursday, 23 July Mr Hayes took home with him a briefcase containing more than £1,878 in wage packets. As his wife went upstairs he put the briefcase on the kitchen table.

A few minutes later, at about 6.30 pm, there was a knock

on the front door and Mrs Hayes called out to her husband to answer it. Almost immediately she heard a shot. As she hurried from a bedroom to the landing a man came running up the stairs, saying, 'Give me that money. I want the money.' 'You haven't killed my husband, have you?' asked the distraught woman. The intruder replied, 'No,' but when Mrs Hayes went downstairs she found her husband lying dead in the hall. As she ran into the kitchen the gunman followed her, hit her on the head with the butt of a revolver, then shot her before snatching up the briefcase and disappearing from the house.

The blow to her head was so vicious that it broke the trigger guard from the revolver. This, left lying on the kitchen floor close to the badly injured wife, was the first of the clues that were to prove the killer's undoing. The second was the bullet that killed Mr Hayes. Ballistics experts were able to tell detectives that the weapon from which the bullet was fired was a snub-nosed .38 Smith and Wesson five-chamber revolver only recently manufactured in the United States. It was not possible to buy one legally in Britain. Detective Superintendent Jack Williams, in charge of the murder hunt, visited the American Embassy in Grosvenor Square, London W1, and was put in touch with Federal Bureau of Investigation agents. They told him that the gun, an unusually compact weapon, was used almost exclusively by gamblers in the States. It was a new model and many had been sold to the bosses of gaming establishments and their croupiers.

The killer had left other clues in the house of death – fingerprints on the newspaper he had used to conceal the gun when Mr Hayes opened the door, and on the handrail of the stairs as he had rushed after Mrs Hayes in his quest for the money. It seemed as if these prints were unlikely to be of immediate help because if, as appeared probable, the crime had been committed by a visiting American gunman, his prints were not likely to be in the Criminal Records Office of Scotland Yard.

But a long, wearisome and painstaking search of more than one hundred thousand sets of prints, each of which had to be compared to those left by the murderer, eventually brought its reward. The incriminating prints were identified as those of Ronald John Cooper, aged twenty-six, whose address was given as Trinity Church Road, Barnes, London SW13. They were on record because he had been sentenced to eighteen months' imprisonment for assault during the Notting Hill race riots a few years earlier.

Superintendent Williams discovered that Cooper, after working as a shop assistant and a car breaker, and serving for a spell in the Merchant Navy, had enrolled at a special 'school' for training croupiers in the West End of London. He had proved an apt pupil and had been offered a job as croupier at the Lucavan Beach Hotel casino in the Bahamas – at a salary of £35 a week and free accommodation. He jumped at the chance and found his new life even more attractive than it had appeared. Tips brought his average salary to £100 weekly, he bought an enormous American car, and often flew to Miami and other millionaires' holiday resorts for week-ends.

With the money came the girls – among them a French 'bunny' called Christine Braun, a New York socialite named Patricia Hartley who owned her own yacht and Cadillac, and Doreen Hunt, who knew Cooper in England before she took an au pair job in New York. It was a wonderful life for the lad from South-West London and it might have stayed that way if he hadn't lost his temper over a trivial incident one night and hit an assistant manager at the casino. He was fired on the spot and given an air-ticket to London. He brought with him the fancy new gun he had bought in Miami.

Within a few days he was virtually penniless. He had been given a £400 pay-off by the casino, but lost the lot in West End gambling clubs. His request for a £20 loan from his bank in London (where he had a credit of eightpence!) was turned down, and on the day following this rebuff Joseph Hayes was shot dead. After the murder Cooper paid £154 in cash for a ticket from London Airport to New York, where he spent a few days with Doreen Hunt before flying on to Nassau in the Bahamas after another job. Superintendent Williams and Detective Inspector Jim Rutland were close behind him. Cooper was extradited from the Bahamas under the Fugitive Offenders Act, and flown back to London with the two officers in the middle of August.

He was charged with the murder of Joseph Hayes, with

wounding Elsie May Hayes with intent to murder, and with robbery with violence. At the Old Bailey in December 1964, before Mr Justice Megaw and an all-male jury, he pleaded not guilty to all charges. There was a dramatic moment when Mrs Hayes was asked if she could recognize the man who killed her husband. Struggling to control her sobs, she pointed a trembling hand at Cooper and said, 'I have no doubt at all that he is the man. I always thought I would be able to recognize him. I just remember his face. I am sure of it. He shot me, too, he shot me. . . .' The bullet Cooper had fired at Mrs Hayes went through her arm into her chest, collapsing one lung, and then lodged in her spine. She had been seriously ill for three months and was still receiving medical treatment at the time of the trial.

Cooper said in the witness-box that he arrived back in England with American dollars worth £450. He had visited gambling clubs but had lost no more than £80 or £90. At the time of the shooting of Mr and Mrs Hayes he was with some friends in Chiswick. He had never been to the Hayes' home and did not possess a gun. The fingerprints found in the murder house were not his prints. On the morning after his visit to Chiswick he decided to return to America and still had £100 left after buying a return air-ticket.

Mrs Eileen Kerr, of Waldeck Road, Chiswick, London W4, called for the defence, said that Ronald Cooper visited her and her husband twice on 23 July, the second time at about 6.45 pm during a television serial called 'Mr Ed', which was about a talking horse. Cooper's words when he left were: 'I do not know when I'll see you again. I might be going abroad tonight.' He had spoken about leaving Britain 'for some excitement'. Mr Phillip Kerr, her husband, told the court that Cooper, whom he had known for eight years, returned to Waldeck Road between 6.30 and 6.45 pm and stayed until about 8.0 pm. Questioned by Mr E. J. P. Cussen for the Crown, Mr Kerr agreed that he previously told the police that Cooper had arrived at his house between 7.0 and 8.0 pm, but at the time he was confused.

Found guilty of capital murder, for which at that time the penalty was execution by hanging, the ex-croupier stood in the dock apparently unmoved as Mr Justice Megaw put on the black cap and spoke the grimly traditional words: 'The sentence of the court is that you suffer death in the manner authorized by law, and may the Lord have mercy on your soul.'

The provisional date for his execution was fixed for 5 January 1965, but later put forward to 27 January. He was the first man to be convicted on a capital charge after Mr Sydney Silverman's Private Members Bill to abolish hanging was introduced into the House of Commons and, because the Bill was at that time being debated and was thought likely to become law, Cooper was reprieved – only five days before he was due to hang – and sentenced to life imprisonment.

In another incident two bullets provided the clue needed by the police to link a suspected man with the murder of his partner in crime. One was in the body of the victim, found in a ditch near Nantwich in Cheshire, and the other was fired into the ceiling of a house near Leeds in Yorkshire – nearly eighty miles away – a month before the killing. Ballistics experts decided that both bullets were fired from the same barrel.

The dead man was John Whyte, a forty-two-year-old ex-seaman and something of a jack of all trades; he was a small-time criminal who had served prison sentences for theft and housebreaking. His body was found on 16 May 1966 by two brothers called Brian and Stanley Harding when they were clipping hedges close to Hurst Green Farm, Norbury, near Nantwich. They thought that they had found a drunk still sleeping off the effects of the night before – until they saw the bullet wounds in his head and chest.

Cheshire police asked Scotland Yard to help in tracing Whyte's movements in the weeks before his death, because it was thought that the crime might be yet another 'vengeance' killing by villains of London's gangland. At that time a special team, headed by the late Detective Chief Superintendent Thomas Butler, was investigating a number of gang murders, including the shooting of George Cornell in the 'Blind Beggar' public house in Whitechapel Road, Stepney, in March 1966 – a murder which was one of the many crimes on the charge sheet when the notorious Kray twins stood trial in

1969. Whyte, it was discovered, had been in London at the end of March, and had hired a Morris 1100 car from a firm in Shepherd's Bush. He was divorced from his wife and had lived for some time in hostels and lodging-houses. He had told a woman friend in his home town of Birkenhead that he was 'in trouble' and she formed the impression that he had double-crossed someone.

It was not much for the police to go on, but it began to look as if the gang-killing theory might be the right one. There was no evidence that Whyte had been killed at the place where the body was found and it was thought probable that he had been shot somewhere else, possibly many miles away, and that his body had been taken by car and dumped in the ditch near Nantwich after dark. He had been dead for at least three days when he was found.

The picture began to change, however, when news of the hired car reached the police. This car had been seen parked without lights at Charing Cross on the evening of 3 May 1966. During the following week a man (not Whyte) and a woman were seen with it on a caravan site at Skegness in Lincolnshire. They had spent nearly two hours cleaning the interior of the vehicle. On 6 June a woman was seen driving it near Doncaster in Yorkshire – and two days later the car was found burning fiercely on waste ground in South London. There was ample evidence that it had been fired deliberately and detectives had little doubt that the purpose of this destruction was to get rid of bloodstains inside – stains which even the earlier careful cleaning had failed to eliminate completely.

The man at Skegness with the car was identified as William John Clarke, aged forty-seven, an itinerant crook who had been in and out of prison since his first conviction for stealing a bicycle when he was twelve years old. He had spent twenty-two of his last twenty-four years in jail, his sentences including ten years' preventive detention at Broadmoor after he had slashed a fellow prisoner with a broken bottle at Walton Prison, Liverpool. His woman companion was forty-year-old Nancy Patricia Hughes, a good-looking brunette who, though born in Cardiff, was nicknamed 'Dublin Pat'. They had known each other for some years and – when not in prison – lived together as man and wife. The couple had not long been out of prison after being sentenced to eighteen months each for post office frauds.

When detectives caught up with them in a hotel in Paddington they found evidence that Clarke and Pat Hughes had lost no time in going back to their life of fraud. They had been travelling all over the country drawing cash from post offices by forging signatures on application forms concerning stolen savings books, but this time there had been a third member of the team – John Whyte. The three of them had worked the racket together for more than two months, making about £50 a week.

The couple were detained in connection with the post office frauds and Clarke was asked by Detective Inspector Kenneth Newton, of Crewe, whether he knew anything about John Whyte's death. 'If I told you what I know about how he got killed I would get the same,' replied Clarke. 'My life would not be worth that,' – he snapped his fingers. He then said that he would tell the detective 'a little allegory' without mentioning names.

'Supposing,' said Clarke, 'you were a wide boy in a hick town up north like Crewe and another bloke like me lived in London and visited Crewe occasionally. You told me you wanted to get into something away from Crewe, perhaps in London with bank books or something. I took you back to London and introduced you to one of the big fellows in Soho, and for a couple of days he sent you out with some books and you were to give him ten per cent. Perhaps you thought you were a bit smarter and would not pay him this ten per cent. He would not say anything. Then you decided to ring the police and split it wide open. . . .' Clarke snapped his fingers again. 'That is what would happen and that is what would happen to me if I told you.'

The police were sure that Clarke himself was the 'big fellow' and that he had killed Whyte because they had quarrelled over the share-out of the money, but there was not enough evidence to bring a murder charge at that stage. There was plenty of evidence of fraud, however, and both Clarke and Pat Hughes were charged with a number of offences. He was sentenced to ten years' imprisonment, which was reduced to seven years on appeal, and she was jailed for two years.

If they thought that was the end of the story they underestimated the tenacity of the police. Detective Chief Superintendent Arthur Benfield, head of Cheshire CID, and a team of officers painstakingly pursued inquiries into the murder of John Whyte – inquiries that were eventually to lead them to a house in Denshaw Drive, Morley, near Leeds. Here they were told of a visit made to the house by Clarke and Dublin Pat about a month before the murder. Clarke had objected to a remark made by another visitor and, by way of registering protest, had taken out a gun and fired a bullet into the ceiling. Detectives sent this bullet for examination by a ballistics expert, who compared it with the bullets taken from Whyte's body. There was no doubt that they had all been fired from the same gun, a .38 British service-type revolver.

Just a year after the killing, in May 1967, William Clarke was charged with murdering John Whyte between 3 and 16 May 1966, and Pat Hughes was charged with harbouring and assisting Clarke knowing that he had murdered Whyte. Both pleaded not guilty when they stood in the dock before Mr Justice Swanwick at Chester Assizes in November 1967, but the jury found Clarke guilty by a majority verdict of ten to two. He was jailed for life. Nancy Patricia Hughes was sentenced to three years' imprisonment for being an accessory after the fact.

William Clarke, like a number of other killers, was a crook with a craving for culture. Almost illiterate when he was sent to Broadmoor earlier in his career of crime, he educated himself at the institution; by the time he was discharged he had become quite an authority on Shakespeare, Shaw and Dickens and could quote long passages from many Greek classics. He wrote poetry, too, and his verses were a regular feature in the *Broadmoor Chronicle*. Nobody really knows why he killed John Whyte, but perhaps the clue is contained in this stanza from one of his own poems:

When reason lags behind impulsive act
Back to time primeval swings the mind;
The body alone cannot counteract
The animal urge that springs from instinct blind.

Murder or accident? That was the question to be decided by a jury when a burglar shot and killed Mr Alfred Bertram Webb, a London accountant and hotel proprietor, as he surprised the intruder in his flat. The case presented itself in 1928, when forensic science was a comparatively elementary business. Nevertheless, it was the evidence provided by a gun and bullets that sent the killer to the gallows.

Middle-aged Mr Webb was a man of regular habits. He normally spent the day at his accountant's office in the City and had dinner at his hotel, the Simla Court in Dawson Place, Bayswater, London W2. Later in the evening he and his wife Ethel and two sons, Clifford, aged twenty-two, and Roy, three years younger, would drive to their luxurious flat at 20 Pembridge Square, just round the corner from Dawson Place.

On 9 February 1928, he varied this routine, calling at the flat at 6.30 pm before going to the hotel because he had some parcels he wanted to leave there. His elder son and a friend, Mr Frank Sweeney, were with him and, as they drew up outside the block, they all noticed lights shining from the Webbs' flat. One of the small panes of frosted glass in the door to the first-floor flat had been broken and when Mr Webb turned his key in the lock he was unable to open the door more than a few inches because the safety chain had been fastened inside. As he peered through the crack of the door they all heard a voice from inside shout 'stick 'em up'.

'Run for the police!' cried Mr Webb. Mr Sweeney and Clifford ran into the street, one turning left and the other right, to find the nearest constable. Clifford had only just left the building when he heard the sound of a shot. He turned and saw a man running from the flats and immediately ran after him, chasing him down Chepstow Place towards Westbourne Grove, but in the dark, slightly foggy evening the pursued man got away.

When Clifford had gone in search of a policeman his father had been bending down trying to peer through the broken glass in the door. Upon his return Clifford found his father lying on the short flight of stairs leading from the flat to the first-floor landing. Blood was pouring from a wound just above

128

his left eye and he was already unconscious. He died in hospital at 2.0 the following morning.

John Horwell, at that time Divisional Detective Inspector in charge of Paddington Division CID, organized the hunt for Mr Webb's murderer. He had little to help him. All he knew was that a short, dark man (the only description Clifford Webb could give) had been seen running from the flats. It was clear that he had been rifling the flat when he was disturbed because several pieces of jewellery were missing, that he had got in by the simple expedient of breaking the glass, putting his hand through and turning the door knob, and that he had shot Mr Webb before running away. He was probably a professional housebreaker and had left no useful fingerprints or anything else to identify him; he could have been one of hundreds of such crooks in the files at Scotland Yard.

The murder weapon was soon found. It had been tossed into the garden of a near-by house. It was a Spanish 25–29 bore gun, which fired a bullet not much larger than those used on miniature rifle ranges; it would have been unlikely to kill unless the bullet had hit a vital spot. But a second cartridge jammed in the breech made it clear to Horwell that the murderer had tried to fire twice and obviously meant to do serious damage. The bullet that had killed Mr Webb by lodging in his brain was a perfect match for the gun and Horwell was convinced that the shot had been fired from inside the flat while Mr Webb was peering through the small aperture in the broken glass.

Knowing the methods of housebreakers – which, incidentally, have not changed much in forty years! – Horwell guessed that the man would have called at several flats or houses that afternoon and early evening. The drill was to ring the doorbell and, if someone answered, ask to speak to Mr Smith or Brown or Jones or use some pretext invented on the spur of the moment. Then, 'Sorry, I must be mistaken' and on to the next place, persisting until one of the chosen addresses proved to be unoccupied. In view of Mr Webb's normal routine the wanted man might have guessed that the flat would be empty, but it seemed unlikely that he would have failed to try a few other places.

Horwell was right. He had. One of the police officers engaged on the laborious task of knocking on every door in that part of Bayswater spoke to a woman who told him that a man had called on the afternoon of 9 February and said, 'May I speak to the chauffeur?' She asked the man where he came from and there was a slight pause before he replied, 'Warwick Garage'. She was able to give a very good description of the caller. There was no Warwick Garage within miles of Bayswater, so it seemed possible that this was the man the police were after. But why should 'Warwick' be the first word that came into his mind? The answer was produced by an inspired guess by Detective Sergeant Welsby. He recalled a flat-breaker named Frederick Stewart living at Warwick Mews in Kensington. Welsby, who knew Stewart well, was given the job of finding him. It did not take him long. Stewart, aged twenty-eight, was a bookmaker's clerk when he wasn't stealing from flats and spent most of his spare time at race-courses and dog-tracks. On 21 February, just twelve days after the murder, Welsby found him in a public house near Southend-on-Sea greyhound-racing stadium.

Stewart admitted readily that he had broken into the flat at Pembridge Square but insisted that the shooting of Alfred Webb was quite accidental. He told Horwell that when he heard voices and realized that he was trapped in the flat he decided to 'make a dash for it'. As he opened the door Mr Webb hit him on the back of the neck, he staggered backwards flinging up his arms, and the pistol was fired accidentally.

It was a good story, but it didn't convince the jury at the Old Bailey when Stewart appeared before Mr Justice Avory in April 1928. Pathological evidence was that the angle at which the bullet penetrated the skull showed it to have been fired downwards – that is, by someone standing upright towards someone in a crouching position. Had Stewart staggered with arms outstretched, as he said, the bullet would have hit the wall.

Stewart was found guilty of murder and sentenced to death. His appeal failed and he was hanged at Pentonville in June 1928 – ironically, on the day of the Derby, an event he had never before missed in the whole of his adult life.

8

Clues so small

To the layman one handful of grit or soil is very much like another. Apart from colour, one human hair differs little from another. Dust and fluff are present in every house and do not, to the naked eye, greatly differ. A thread of wool or cotton is recognizable by colour but appears to have no outstanding characteristics. But when any of these items are placed beneath the sophisticated microscopes in a modern forensic science laboratory each can tell its own story.

Every single hair, for instance, is made up of three parts – the cuticle, or outer skin, bearing a pattern of tiny scales; the cortex, which contains the natural colouring; and the medulla, which is really the pith of the hair. Bleaching, cutting, tinting and different types of permanent waving leave their own 'trade marks' and all help, by matching up with hair from a murder victim or a criminal who has visited the scene of a crime, to establish identification.

The dye of any fabric is much more significant than it appears because even an apparently uniform colour can show great variations of shade, just as irregularities of weave, indiscernible to the naked eye, are clear to a trained microscopist. Any sample of soil or household dust may contain a dozen or more separate ingredients. The proportions of one to the other are often vitally important when a specimen taken from the scene of a crime is compared to one from the clothing or home of a suspected person.

A new grey worsted suit, a floral-patterned artificial-silk slip and a few grains of sandy soil all helped to hang the killer of Ruby Annie Keen. As in many other cases in which the microscope has been used to help the course of justice, not one of these seemingly trivial items would have been sufficient to justify a conviction, but added together, and combined with the rest of the evidence, they were enough to convince a jury that a verdict of guilty was the right one.

Ruby Keen was a factory worker. In her home town of Leighton Buzzard in Bedfordshire, where she lived in Plantation Road, she was often described as 'looking like a film star'. She was certainly a very pretty girl and always followed the cosmetic fashions of the day – carefully waved hair, bright red Cupid's bow lips and a discreet touch of mascara to emphasize her sparkling eyes. All these were the hallmarks of the smart 1930s girl, and Ruby was a thoroughly modern miss.

Even while still a schoolgirl she had plenty of admirers and soon she was able to pick and choose among the young men anxious to date her. In 1931, when fair-haired Ruby was seventeen, she met a tall, good-looking young man named Leslie George Stone, a year her senior, who lived about two miles away in the village of Heath and Reach. They were mutually attracted and for some months spent most of their free time together. When Leslie joined the army they exchanged affectionate letters and resumed their romantic relationship during his periods at home.

Then, about a year after their first date, Leslie was posted to Hong Kong. He saw Ruby on his embarkation leave and they promised to write to each other. They did correspond – for two years. But Ruby was young and attractive and, particularly as she was not engaged to Stone, saw no reason why she should not enjoy other male companionship while he was away. Inevitably her letters to Stone became less frequent and finally she ceased writing. He sent her a few more letters and then apparently lost interest.

At home in Leighton Buzzard Ruby led a harmlessly gay life with plenty of social outings and a variety of boyfriends, among them at least two policemen. Eventually it was a police officer to whom she became engaged and in the spring of 1937 they were making plans for a June wedding when Leslie Stone reappeared on the scene.

He had discharged himself from the army and was working as a quarry labourer near his home. Nobody knows whether or not he would have taken the initiative in seeking out his former girlfriend, but there is no doubt that his interest was revived when he saw her – then twenty-three and even more desirable as a young woman than she had been as a girl – walking along Leighton Buzzard High Street with a handsome, hefty young man. Stone did not speak and crossed the road to avoid being seen, but he began to keep a look-out for her and a few days later met her again. She was walking alone.

He asked why she had stopped writing to him and she pointed out that five years was a very long time. She told him that there had been other boyfriends and that she was now engaged to a policeman. In a kindly way she said she hoped that they would continue to be friends and agreed that there would be no harm in spending one evening together 'for old times' sake'.

The date was fixed for Sunday 11 April 1937. Stone bought a new suit with £3 17s army reserve pay and wore it for the first time that evening. Ruby, smart in a sophisticated yellow dress, with a black and white scarf knotted casually round her neck, met him in the saloon bar of the Golden Bell Hotel in Leighton Buzzard. They stayed there talking for a while and then went on to the 'Cross Keys' public house, which they did not leave until closing time at 10.0 pm. No less than eleven people in those two pubs heard Stone pleading with Ruby Keen to give up her policeman fiancé and marry him instead. Two of them were so intrigued by these romantic overtones to the normal bar gossip that they followed at a discreet distance when the couple left the 'Cross Keys'. They later told the police that the couple had walked to Ruby's home, paused for a few moments outside the old stone cottage, and then walked on towards a secluded coppice known as 'the firs'.

Ruby was not seen alive again. Early next morning a farmworker found her body lying underneath a tall fir tree. Her yellow dress had been ripped right down the front. She had been raped and then strangled with her own scarf. She had obviously fought hard because the ground had been scuffed and trodden. As soon as the body had been removed police officers took plaster casts of confused footprints, some small and obviously made by the girl's high-heeled shoes, some made by a man's shoes. There were also two clear indentations made by the knees of the killer as he knelt beside his

133

victim. The plaster cast of the knee prints later became an exhibit in the Black Museum of Scotland Yard and is always shown to young recruits to teach them how important it is never to disturb anything at the scene of a crime. In view of Ruby Keen's romantic association with the police force, the footprints of any police officer at the scene of the murder could have led to unutterable confusion and might well have resulted in suspicion falling on the wrong man.

Leslie Stone and Ruby had been seen by so many people in the two public houses that he was an obvious suspect, but he was not the only one. Detective Chief Inspector William Barker, of Scotland Yard's murder squad, sent detectives to seek out every snapshot of Ruby with a male companion. All these men and boys were traced and interviewed, including, of course, her police officer fiancé and other policemen with whom she had been friendly. This was particularly important because a married couple taking a short cut home on the night of the murder said that at 10.30 pm they had seen, near the spot where Ruby's body was found, a girl in the arms of a man wearing a blue uniform with silver buttons.

All these suspects were eventually eliminated. Stone, when interviewed by detectives, admitted readily that he had spent the evening with Ruby, but said that he had left her near Plantation Road at about 10.15 pm.

Chief Inspector Barker asked for the suit and shoes worn by Stone on 11 April and both were sent for microscopic examination at the Yard. The late Detective Inspector Fred Cherrill, of the Fingerprint Department, compared the shoes with the plaster-cast footmarks, but was able to say only that they were of approximately the same size and that in each case the heel of the right shoe was worn down. Upon examining the plaster-cast marks of the murderer's knees, he found that it was possible to discern the pattern of the cloth. The weave was identical with that of Stone's suit, but as it was a cheap suit made of commonplace cloth and identical with hundreds worn in Leighton Buzzard, this did no more than establish that the kneeprints *could* have been made by Stone. This finding eliminated the possibility that the marks were created by a policeman's uniform – doubly important because of the girl's connection with the force and the evidence of the couple who thought they had seen a policeman and a girl near the scene of the crime. The weave was totally dissimilar from that of the worsted trousering of the Bedfordshire Constabulary.

It was noticed, too, that although Stone's suit was obviously new, the knees of the trousers had been brushed so vigorously that the nap of the cloth had worn quite thin. Even so the microscope revealed a few grains of soil still embedded in the knees – and it was soil that exactly matched the samples of mixed brown clay and sharp crystalline sand that had been taken from the ground beneath and round Ruby's body.

Ironically, it was an over-zealous attempt to rid the suit of all traces of the crime that led to the discovery of the next clue. A tiny thread of artificial silk had been brushed right into the cloth of the jacket and micro-chemical tests on the dye of this thread showed it to be identical with fibres from the slip worn by Ruby on the day of her killing.

Detective Chief Inspector Barker went to see Stone and found him among a group of friends. They were all talking about the murder and when Barker said he wanted to talk to Stone one of the other men commented: 'No need to worry Leslie. Everyone knows that Ruby had long fingernails and the man who attacked her was bound to have his face and hands badly scratched.' Stone virtually signed his own death warrant as he unthinkingly retorted: 'Oh, but she had her gloves on.' He was charged with murder and appeared before Lord Hewart, then the Lord Chief Justice, at the Old Bailey in June 1937.

A scientific witness was closely cross-examined by defence counsel about the thread of artificial silk found on the jacket. Was it certain that this thread actually came from Ruby Keen's underslip? The witness replied: 'No. The fibre which I found on the prisoner's jacket is an artificial silk fibre mainly white but upon which there are four different dyes. This fibre is similar in all respects to the fibre of the undergarment and the four dyes on the fibre are identical to the dyes of a floral pattern on the underslip. I am able to say that this fibre could have come from the dead girl's underwear.'

In the face of the evidence, Stone changed his story when he stood in the witness-box. He said that he and Ruby had walked up the lane together and had quarrelled. 'She struck me,' he said. 'I caught hold of her scarf, I think, and pulled it. I think I knotted it again after that. I was in a kind of rage.' He added that he thought he had just stunned her. He did not think she was dead or badly injured. Under cross-examination he admitted that he had decided he could not stick to his original story after hearing the evidence about his suit.

Addressing the jury, Lord Hewart said that with a person who had proved himself so clever in the fabrication of a falsehood they might ask what part, if any, of this story he was now telling they could trust, unless it was corroborated by other testimony.

After the jury had been out for some time they sent this question in writing to Lord Hewart: 'If, as the result of an intention to commit rape, a girl is killed – although there is no intention to kill her – is a man guilty of murder?' Lord Hewart replied: 'Yes, undoubtedly.'

Stone was found guilty. An appeal was lodged on the grounds of misdirection, the defence maintaining that the answer to the jury's question was inadequate. The appeal, however, was dismissed. Leslie George Stone was hanged at Pentonville on Friday 13 August 1937.

Ruby Keen's policeman fiancé resigned from the force before Stone's trial began. So, too, did another policeman with whom she was known to have enjoyed a flirtatious relationship.

When an eight-year-old girl is found murdered with severe genital injuries, the natural assumption is that she has been the victim of a rapist. It appeared that this had been the fate of little Helen Priestly, only child of John Dean Priestly, a house-painter, and his wife Agnes, who lived in a two-roomed tenement flat in Urquhart Road, Aberdeen in Scotland.

After her midday dinner on 20 April 1934 Helen was sent to the local bakery to buy a loaf. She was due back at school at 2.0, so when she had not returned home with the bread by that time her mother was naturally worried. Mrs Priestly inquired at the shop and was told that Helen had left the premises clutching the bread and the voucher slip recording the purcase. Had she gone straight to school? No. She had not been seen there since leaving after the morning session.

Mrs Priestly searched the streets and then contacted her husband. Before 3.0 pm the police knew that the girl was missing and at 6.0 that evening a nine-year-old boy volunteered the information that he had seen Helen being dragged up the street on to a tram by a middle-aged man wearing a dark coat. Descriptions of the man and child were broadcast and messages were flashed onto cinema screens. The whole area was searched by police officers, friends and relatives of the Priestlys and hundreds of civilian volunteers. More than two thousand people were questioned. Derelict buildings, parks, open spaces and waste ground were thoroughly scoured.

There was no clue to the whereabouts of the missing child and at midnight the Priestlys and their neighbours were persuaded to go home for a few hours' rest. Mr Alexander Porter, who lived opposite the Priestlys, left his bed at 4.30 next morning to continue the search. As he opened the door of the tenement-house he saw something in a dark corner of the lobby. It was a sack. From it the legs of a child were protruding.

Helen Priestly had been strangled and apparently sexually assaulted. She was fully dressed except for her knickers and school beret. The sack contained a handful of cinders – one was lodged between the dead girl's teeth and others were in her hair – and dust, fluff and human and animal hair. Shortly before midnight, only a few hours previously, when the staircase, back-yard and communal lavatories of the tenement-house had been searched there was no sign of the sack, with its pathetic contents. Detectives were puzzled. Why should her murderer have risked discovery by returning the victim to her own doorstep?

The lad who said that he had seen Helen taken away was asked if he could give a more detailed description of her abductor. To the consternation of the police, he burst into tears. 'I never saw her at all,' he sobbed. 'I made it all up.' This confession at least helped to explain some puzzling features. Although there had been a great deal of activity in Urquhart Road throughout the night, nobody had seen a man carrying a sack. It was a very wet night, yet both the sack and the child's body were quite dry. The inference was plain. Helen had been killed inside the building, her body kept in one of the flats, then quickly dumped in the lobby some time in the early hours of the morning when the searchers had temporarily retired.

It was estimated that the girl had been dead for between fourteen and fifteen hours before her body was found, and two witnesses came forward rather belatedly with information which helped to confirm the time. Another child reported having seen Helen, carrying the bread and walking towards her home, at approximately 1.45 pm on 20 April. A slater working nearby said he had heard a scream 'like a frightened child' coming from the tenement-house at about 2.0 pm that day, but had not thought it serious enough to merit investigation. Every man living in the building was questioned and all seemed to have watertight alibis.

Then, when the full results of the post-mortem examination reached detectives, the whole direction of the inquiry changed. Dr Robert Richards and Professor Shennan, pathologist at Aberdeen University, told the police: 'This is not a case of rape.' The injuries to the child's sexual organs had been inflicted before death, but had not been caused in the usual way by a male. They had been made by some sharp instrument such as a poker or porridge stick (used for stirring the traditional Scottish breakfast food) and could therefore have been inflicted equally by a man or woman.

The detectives returned to the tenement-house, this time to question every woman living there. Among them was Mrs Jeannie Ewen Donald, an attractive woman of thirty-eight, who lived with her husband Alexander and nine-year-old daughter, also named Jeannie, in one of the two ground-floor flats, just below the Priestlys. The Donalds 'kept themselves to themselves' and Mrs Donald and Mrs Priestly had not been on speaking terms for some years. The Donalds, in fact, were the only people in the tenement-house who had not joined in the search for Helen when she was reported missing.

Mrs Donald gave a clear account of her movements on 20 April. She told the police that she had gone shopping at about 1.15, detailed the shops visited and quoted prices paid. She had returned home at 2.15 and had spent most of the afternoon ironing dresses for her daughter to wear at a dancing-school rehearsal that evening. A check on the prices that she said she had paid in the market for eggs and oranges revealed, however, that they were the prices being asked during the previous week and were not accurate for 20 April. A shop selling dress materials which she was supposed to have visited was in fact closed on 20 April, and fabrics that she said she had examined had been sold out earlier that week.

In the Donalds' flat the police discovered nine sacks. Five of them had a hole in the corner similar to a hole in the murder sack. Three also had black marks – caused by standing saucepans on them. The sack in which Helen was found had similar marks. All these circumstances were suspicious, but nothing more. The link between Jeannie Donald and Helen Priestly was established in the laboratories of Edinburgh University, where Sir Sydney Smith, Professor of Forensic Medicine, carried out an examination of the debris in the sack in which the child's body was found.

The cinders revealed very little, apart from the fact that they were washed cinders – Mrs Donald was the only person in the tenement-house known to wash cinders and evidence of this was found in the waste-pipe trap of her sink. The fluff in the sack was far more rewarding. Under the microscope it was shown to be made up of no less than two hundred different substances, including wool, cotton, silk and linen in six different colours, some undyed textiles, as well as cat and rabbit hairs and some human hair.

Using a comparison microscope, which enables the microscopist to examine two sets of fibres at the same time, these materials were separated and compared to the components of a random sample of household fluff taken from the Donalds' flat. Twenty-five different fibres matched exactly; so did the cat and rabbit hairs. The human hairs from the sack were rather coarse in texture and were oddly twisted in a way that suggested unskilled permanent waving. Under the comparison microscope they appeared to be identical with hairs taken from Mrs Donald's brush. Samples of fluff taken from all the other flats in the tenement were subjected to similar tests, but none matched the fluff from the death sack.

Bloodstains of Group O, the same as that of the dead child, were found on a soapflakes packet, a scrubbing brush and a washing-up cloth in Mrs Donald's kitchen. These articles were sent to the department of bacteriology at Edinburgh University and compared to bloodstains on Helen's combinations. Because of the nature of the child's injuries, her blood had become contaminated with a form of intestinal bacteria – and the same bacteria was revealed in the blood on the washing-up cloth.

Sir Sydney Smith and his university colleagues spent six weeks on these and many other tests, eventually producing 253 items of evidence for the trial of Jeannie Donald.

Both she and her husband were at first charged jointly with the murder of Helen Priestly, but Alexander Donald was released from custody after it had been established beyond doubt that at the time of the murder he was in the hairdressing salon where he was employed. Jeannie Donald stood her trial alone and was found guilty by the jury at the High Court of Edinburgh after an absence of only eighteen minutes. She was sentenced to death, but this was later commuted to penal servitude for life.

The motive for the murder was never explained. The two families were not good friends and Helen appeared to have annoyed Mrs Donald by calling her 'coconut' – presumably a reference to her badly permed hair – and by ringing her doorbell as she passed the Donald flat on her way upstairs. A number of possible motives have been put forward, but the most likely one was that suggested by Sir Sydney Smith in a newspaper article many years later.

An incidental discovery at the post-mortem examination showed that Helen suffered from an overgrowth of lymphatic tissue, a condition which would cause her to faint more easily than a normal child. Mrs Donald perhaps shook the child rather roughly because she had been cheeky, or had once again rung the door bell; the girl lost consciousness and Mrs Donald thought that she had died. The woman then tried to make it look like a rape case, but Helen regained consciousness and screamed. She was strangled when Mrs Donald put her hands round her neck in an attempt to quieten her.

If this was the true story, Jeannie Donald might have pleaded culpable homicide (manslaughter in an English court) which the Crown was prepared to accept. The defence refused to use the loophole, convinced there would be a not guilty verdict on the greater charge.

After more than ten years in prison Mrs Donald was released on parole to look after her husband, who had been given only a few months to live. When he died she was allowed to keep her freedom. She changed her name, got a job and eventually remarried. When last heard of she was living a peaceful life somewhere in Scotland.

Mabel Tattershaw was a most unlikely candidate for murder. Aged forty-eight, she was small and unattractive, and always shabbily dressed in cast-off clothes given to her by neighbours. With a husband in prison, she took in lodgers to keep the home going for herself and two teenage daughters and her life of poverty and grinding hard work showed in the greying hair, set lips and roughened red hands. A woman of little personality – so negative that she had few friends and no enemies – her only pleasure was escape into the world of make-believe whenever she could afford the price of a seat at the cinema.

Yet it was largely because she was so ordinary that she was killed. She became the 'perfect victim' for a man who was seeking to commit the 'perfect murder'. Ironically, too, it was her one escape route from life – the cinema – that led to her death. On the evening of 2 August 1951 she thankfully left her home at Longmead Drive, Sherwood, Nottingham, and, accompanied by one of her lodgers, Mrs Lily Wilson, settled into the cheapest part of the Roxy Cinema. There, to heighten the romance unfolded on the screen, she found a little excitement of her own in the darkness of the auditorium. She got into conversation with the man sitting in the seat beside her. Nobody will ever really know who made the first approach, but Lily Wilson later said that she noticed Mrs Tattershaw whispering to this man. Certainly they arranged to meet outside the local Metropole Cinema at 6.0 the following evening, and before leaving home to keep this 'date' Mabel Tattershaw made herself as attractive as she knew how in a second-hand plum-coloured floral dress and borrowed plastic beads. Her fourteen-year-old daughter, who was told 'No', when she asked if she could go too, was surprised to see her mother using face-powder and lipstick – something she rarely bothered to do.

She left home somewhere between 5.0 and 6.0 on Friday 3 August 1951, to keep the appointment she had made in the dim light of the cinema, and it is difficult to assess who was most shocked when the couple came face to face in bright daylight. *She* saw a weedy, pasty-faced youth of nineteen with pale blue eyes and a long, thin face made even more elongated by his already receding fair hair. *He* discovered that his new lady-friend was a pathetic little drab woman who looked almost too old to be his mother.

They were seen together by Miss Beryl Kingstone, a telegraphist, of Butler Terrace, Hall Street, Sherwood, and later – between 6.0 and 7.0 pm – by William Barry Cox, of the RAF, from Dereham in Norfolk, who thought that they were mother and son.

Mrs Tattershaw did not return home that night and on the following day, Saturday 4 August, her daughter reported her to the police as missing. Nothing more was heard of her until 11.30 am on 9 August when the late Norman Rae, chief crime reporter of the *News of the World,* sitting in his London office, received a telephone call from Nottingham. A male voice asked him: 'What would you pay for the exclusive story and pictures of a murder?' Rae, who, like all other Fleet Street crime men, is only too accustomed to calls from time-wasting cranks and people who hope to get paid for what is often false or useless information, asked brightly: 'Is this a murder you've done or one you're going to do?'

The man replied that this was a murder he had discovered the previous day, a woman strangled in a wood outside Nottingham, and suggested that the *News of the World* might like to take pictures and then tell the police, getting the credit for discovering the body.

Rae kept the man talking while a colleague contacted Nottingham police and the CID arrived while the caller was still in the public kiosk from which he was making the call. The man, Leonard Herbert Mills, aged nineteen, lived with his father, a miner, and stepmother, at Mansfield Street, Nottingham. Without hesitation he took the police officers to a lonely, overgrown orchard – known locally as 'the jungle' – near Sherwood Vale. There, in an eight-foot-deep gully, they found the body of Mabel Tattershaw. She had died by manual

142

strangulation and there were a number of bruises on her body, some caused before and some after death. Mills handed the police a plastic necklace he said he had found near the body. Mills, of course, was closely questioned. He was an odd youth with apparently only three, widely divergent, interests in life – reading and writing poetry, gambling and the study of crime. He had been some trouble to his father, refusing to work after one short spell as a dispatch clerk, and relying on heavy betting to make enough money for his needs. He had in fact won £3,800 on one horse race when he was only seventeen, but had lost it within a few weeks. At the time of Mabel Tattershaw's murder, he owed one Nottingham bookmaker no less than £1,000.

He was an obvious suspect for the murder, but at the outset of the inquiry there was no evidence on which to hold him, and by the time the Fleet Street reporters arrived in Nottingham he was ready, in fact eager, to hold a press conference. He told the pressmen that he went to the orchard in Sherwood Vale to read poetry – he took a book of Shelley with him – and had noticed the body when he bent down to pick up the plastic beads. He realized that he might be charged with the woman's murder, but he would not mind that because when he was subsequently acquitted 'there was bound to be a lot of money in it.' He said that he knew newspapers paid high prices for the life stories of people who had been acquitted of murder.

What Mills did not know at that time was that two clues had been found which could tie him in with the murder. When detectives were examining his clothing he made an arrogant bet with them – £1 for every spot of blood they found. They found no blood, nor anything on his clothing or his person to involve him with Mrs Tattershaw. But examination of the dead woman and her clothes yielded the two vital clues which allied her to Mills. From her old brown coat Professor J. M. Webster, Home Office pathologist, picked two hairs which had definitely not come from Mabel Tattershaw's head. They were, said Professor Webster, from the head of a fair-haired young man who used a vegetable-oil hair dressing – and they exactly matched hairs taken from Mills's pocket comb.

Scrapings from under the dead woman's fingernails failed

to reveal the scraps of skin or blood that might have been expected if she had scratched her attacker in an attempt to defend herself, but the badly roughened hands yielded something else – a tiny thread of blue wool fibre of the same material as the suit Mills had been wearing on 3 August.

When Mills first spoke to Norman Rae he had said that he thought his information was worth £1,000 but that he was prepared to accept £250. He was given £80 by the *News of the World* in return for his story of the discovery of the body. He made a romantically worded statement in which he said that he had had a sonnet 'buzzing in his brain' and was looking for somewhere quiet where he could put it down on paper. After finding the body he went away and sat on a bank to think, during which time he read one of Shelley's three poems entitled 'Death'.

Mills stuck to his story about the discovery of the body when the inquest on Mrs Tattershaw was opened at Nottingham on 13 August. The deputy coroner, Mr A. G. Rothera, asked him three times if he was sure it was on Wednesday 8 August that he found the body, and each time Mills replied, 'Yes.' In answer to further questions he said that the body was lying face downwards with a coat over it. He was at the murder scene for about five minutes but did not touch the body, put anything on it or take anything from it.

Mr Rothera: 'Why did you not approach the police or my office?'

Mills: 'In the beginning I did not want to risk being involved. I thought of leaving it and not saying anything. Then I waited until I had given details to the paper.'

'You had it in mind to sell the information?' – 'Yes. If I was going to get involved at all I might as well profit by it.'

'Were you conscious of the increased difficulties that would result from the police not having this information?' – 'Not greatly. I was thinking more of being involved myself.'

Asked if he had touched the body, Mills replied that he could not have touched it without going down the gully and that he had stayed on top.

Professor Webster gave evidence that Mrs Tattershaw had been strangled and had apparently also been punched. The body had been either dragged or pushed along the ground.

144

When he made his examination on 10 August she had been dead at least forty-eight hours and probably for six days.

Mills continued to talk freely to anyone who would listen, insisting that he could see from the top of the gully that the woman had been strangled. He did not know that Professor Webster, expert in such matters, had been unable to tell from that position – eight feet above the body – that strangulation had, in fact, been the cause of death. Even before the inquest Mills was anxious to air this knowledge and was contemptuous of early newspaper reports that Mabel Tattershaw had been battered to death. On one occasion he flung a newspaper down in front of a group of reporters, declaring: 'Newspaper reporters are just fools. She had no head injuries. You will find that she was strangled.' The police, he added, had a very fine record, but this time they had met their Waterloo because they would never find the murderer.

Still free, and confident that he would remain so, Mills continued to contact Norman Rae, promising that he had more vital and sensational evidence for which he wanted payment. Eventually, at Mills's request, Rae met him in a Nottingham hotel on 24 August 1951. There Mills wrote a confession to the crime, which was handed to Detective Superintendent Ellington, head of Nottingham CID.

This was Mills's statement: 'I was sitting in the Roxy Cinema. Two women later entered, sitting beside me in the same row. One woman endeavoured to make conversation. Not wishing to be impolite I answered, trying hard to make it clear that I did not wish it. She persisted, at one period she was a little suggestive. She invited me to see her the following day. I refused. She persisted.

'I had always considered the possibility of the perfect crime – murder. I am very much interested in crime. Here was my opportunity. I have been most successful. No motive, no clues. Why, if I had not reported finding the body I should not have been connected in any manner whatsoever. I am quite proud of my achievement.

'Seeing the possibility of putting my theory into practice I consented to meeting her on the morrow. I met her the following day, Friday.

'We walked, eventually coming out opposite the Wood-

145

thorpe Post Office. As we did so, a former school friend of mine, Barry Cox, observed me. He was not the only one. Upon the other side I was seen by two girls, one of whom I know to be Beryl Kingstone. I then proceeded with this woman by a road alongside Woodthorpe Park. I went through the rose gardens at the rear of the park, proceeded along a path which brought me to the road leading down to and passing by the orchard. Walking up a path we branched off to the right.

'She took off her coat and lay down. I asked could I have the beads she wore. I was interested in plastic, or rather I thought they might interfere with my little crime and intentions. She broke the beads from her neck to give to me. I tied them. She was a very simple woman.

'We had spoken on the way there and she had told me of her husband being in prison, also of her daughter having been seduced by the lodger. She had known something of what her daughter was doing, yet did not attempt to interfere in any way. If I had thought of changing my mind, the thought of the daughter quickly altered it. I did not like what had happened. I was satisfied I had found the perfect victim.

'She said she was cold. I had not interfered with her in any way, nor did I. I covered her with her own coat, then my own coat. She had her eyes closed. I put on a pair of gloves. I knelt with my knees upon her shoulders. The coats were placed upon her so that she would not clutch or gather any thread within her finger nails.

'I was very pleased. I think I did it rather well. The strangling itself was quite easily accomplished. I am right-handed and I applied most pressure to the right hand side of her neck. I examined the contents of her pockets, which I replaced. I slid her down the bank, covered the coat over her, then left, arriving home at, I think, 9.20 pm.

'I have determined to make this statement, which I realise involves a charge of murder. I now confess I murdered Mrs Tattershaw.'

Mills was, of course, arrested and charged with Mabel Tattershaw's murder, but he remained quite unconcerned because he was convinced that no jury would convict him. Having made his confession, he planned to retract it at his trial so that when, as he thought, he was acquitted, he would be able to demand vast sums of money from newspapers who would be competing for his story.

He did, in fact, retract his confession when he stood in the witness box at Nottingham Assizes, before Mr Justice Byrne, during his four-day trial at the end of November 1951. He prefaced his account of the events concerning Mrs Tattershaw by saying that his mother died while he was a child. He began to take an interest in poetry when he was fifteen and had since read a lot; he had also written poetry. While he was not working he obtained money from betting on horses.

On 2 August, he said, he went to the Roxy Cinema and the woman sitting beside him got into conversation and suggested a future meeting. At first he refused, but she was very persuasive and eventually he agreed. He had no idea what she looked like and when he met her the following evening he was shocked to see how old and shabby she was: 'I was ashamed to be seen walking with her, so I said, more or less, that I had made a mistake and had better go. She walked away and I went round the corner and got a bus to the Scala Cinema.'

Five days later he went to the orchard to read Shelley's poems and, after picking up a string of plastic beads, he saw the body of a woman lying in the gully. He was shocked to realize that it was the woman he had met outside the Metropole Cinema. He went home to think things over and decided that he would turn his discovery to profit, so telephoned the *News of the World* to offer them his information. Most of the money paid to him by the newspaper went on gambling and he lost £60 on one bet. He then decided that he would confess to the murder of Mrs Tattershaw, although he realized that he was running risks by doing so, but he was a gambler and took a chance. The confession was not true. He thought that if he was charged and the charges were withdrawn, or he was found not guilty, it would be of value and he could turn it to profit.

Mr R. C. Vaughan KC, prosecuting, spoke of 'trafficking in corpses' and cross-examined Mills on why he did not report his discovery to the police before telephoning the newspaper. 'Do you really want the jury to think you are a monster?' asked Mr Vaughan, and Mills replied: 'The jury are entitled to think what they like.'

'You want us to believe that your avarice for money is such that you will stop at nothing?' – 'Yes.'

'Even now you have no regret whatever that you tried to make money out of this corpse?' – 'No.'

'Did it occur to you that this woman was lying there all this time with her relations not knowing where she was? Are you sorry now?' – 'No.'

'Do you not think it was cruel?' – 'Once a person's dead it makes no difference.'

While Mills was in jail awaiting trial he wrote a letter to a friend, a nurse named June Brown, in which he said: 'If certain people will come forward and speak the truth I shall probably be acquitted. If not, it is quite possible I might hang. It has not yet been decided whether I plead guilty or not guilty. I may take the risk of pleading guilty.' Reading part of this letter in court, Mr Vaughan asked Mills: 'Was this another gambler's risk?' Mills replied: 'There might be more money in it.' Mr Vaughan then read a verse that was included in the letter:

Though so many would believe
This tale is most untrue,
Who sells the news on Saturday
On Friday that he slew.

Mills replied 'No' when Mr Vaughan put it to him that he had in fact murdered Mrs Tattershaw on 3 August. 'Finding that the body had not been discovered for five days, you conceived the villainous scheme of turning it to profit, for which to this day you are not ashamed?' continued Mr Vaughan.

'I am not ashamed to profit out of it' retorted Mills.

Sidney James Cantrell, a probation officer, told the court that he had known Mills for two years and assessed him as 'a most unusual individual'.

'He is extraordinarily self-confident, partly because of his betting successes,' said Mr Cantrell. 'He is very selfish, dislikes work, and seems incapable of deep affection.'

Further evidence of Mills's unusual character was given by Dr Richard Russell Prewer, medical officer of Lincoln Prison, who said that the young man's curious unconcern was too

148

consistent to be purely assumed. He liked showing off and drawing attention to himself and three incidents while he was in prison demonstrated his callousness. The first occurred when his grandmother wrote to say that she was praying for him; Mills replied that he would prefer a cake to prayers. The second occurred when his father and stepmother travelled from Nottingham to Lincoln to visit him and he refused to see them. The third was the 'very malicious' crushing of a warder's arm in the door of his cell. Dr Prewer said that the murder of Mrs Tattershaw bore some characteristics of the sadist, but he thought it improbable that Mills was a sadist. He did not think that Mills was suffering from any defect of reason because of a disease of the mind. He was aware of what he was doing.

Mr Richard Elwes KC, counsel for Leonard Mills, who described his client as 'a hateful boy' and 'this idiot boy', said that the alleged confession was 'sheer invention, full of bombast and childish vanity, obviously fed on cheap fiction'. Mills made it with the indecent object of trying to make money. His character was a mixture of grossness and a longing for something spiritual. On one side was his preoccupation with money in its most filthy aspect; on the other a struggle, probably quite subconscious and not recognized by him for what it was, for something beautiful and pure. Mr Elwes read to the court this poem, said to have been written by Mills:

From your eyes there is no succour,
I am quite helpless in your power,
Dearest, fairest, is this your hour?
Do not my heart deny
For by the power of your eye
I am doomed to live or die.
All is yours I have to give,
You are all for which I care to live;
To thee I pledge to constant be,
I love thee to eternity.

'Was this written by a vicious ruffian?' asked Mr Elwes. 'This murder was obviously a sadist's murder. Whoever killed Mabel Tattershaw did so for some perverted reason. Whatever else may be said about Mills, he is not a sadist.'

Mr Elwes turned to the jury and asked: 'How did Mills know the woman had been strangled?' He went on: 'This strange youth, with Shelley in one hand and the *News of the World* in the other, answered that nine out of ten murdered women are strangled. Uppermost in his mind was the lust for money—easy money. Second was his love of the limelight. You are seeing it now. Did you ever see anybody enjoying so complacently being the cynosure of all eyes, even though the eyes are riveted upon him in utter disgust? It is the composure of the gambler who has staked a heavy stake and is awaiting the issue with utter composure.

'If you are ever going to see a man who has gambled for his life, and is composed as to whether he wins or loses, you have seen one now. That is the character who has made the confession which I persist in submitting to you is a bogus confession.'

The jury took only twenty-five minutes to reach their verdict of guilty. No one can say that the confession alone, which in view of Mills's peculiar character might have been bogus, would have been enough to ensure that verdict. Equally, it is impossible to say that without the confession, the evidence of the hairs and the scrap of blue wool – which could have got on to Mrs Tattershaw's clothing during the brief period in which Mills admitted being with the woman – would have been regarded as irrefutable evidence of guilt. It was the two together that persuaded the jury of his guilt and brought a death sentence from the judge. After an unsuccessful appeal, Leonard Mills was executed at Lincoln jail on 11 December 1951.

Signs of blood

'Tell-tale bloodstains' was a cliché to which old-style thriller writers were unashamedly faithful and, hackneyed though the description may be, they had every excuse to use it. It is factually accurate. Blood *does* tell tales. It can sometimes tell almost the whole story of a crime.

Blood splashes at the scene of a murder or assault can give a lot of immediate information. They can show the respective positions of victim and attacker, the distance between the two and the direction from which blows were aimed, to what extent the injured person tried to counter the attack, and whether the blood on the clothes of the killer is likely to be in the form of smears or splashes. Even quite small drops of blood can be informative because their differing shapes indicate, within twenty inches, the height from which they fell.

But it is the identification of blood groups that has proved of the greatest value in solving crimes of violence and this is an area of forensics in which tremendous advances have been made in recent years. One of the pioneers is Dr Margaret Pereira, top blood-group expert at Scotland Yard's Forensic Laboratory, who in the early 1960s discovered a revolutionary new technique in blood-group identification. Dr Pereira, who joined the Yard's laboratory staff when she left her convent school in 1948, led a team of biologists in devising a system which makes it possible to isolate a much wider range of blood-groups than hitherto and enables analysis to be made of a spot no bigger than a pin-head. Before these discoveries bloodstains on clothing and other articles could be classified only as belonging to one of the four main groups – O, the blood group of forty-seven per cent of people in Great Britain; A (forty-two per cent); B (eight per cent) and AB (three per cent). Many sub-divisions of these primary groups are now identifiable.

Research on this project is still continuing, and it is estimated that within the next ten years a sample of blood will be as significant as a fingerprint – identifiable as belonging to one person and to that one person alone.

The Pereira Test, as it is now known, was used for the first time in October 1966, when blood samples were taken from all the men of Beenham, the Berkshire village which was the scene of the murder of a children's nurse named Yolande Waddington. That murder remains unsolved. But sixteen months later Margaret Pereira was again involved in a murder case, the brutal killing of Claire Josephs, and this time with positive results.

There seemed no reason at all why anyone should want to kill this girl. She was young, pretty and popular, happy in her job as a telephone operator and happier still at home with her husband Bernard, to whom she had been married for only five months. She was a girl apparently without an enemy in the world. Yet, just after 8.0 on the bleak night of 7 February 1968 she was found in their flat at Deepdene Court, Kingswood Road, Shortlands, Kent, with her throat cut and four stab wounds in her body. She had not been sexually assaulted and nothing had been stolen from the premises. It was seemingly a killing without reason.

The lack of a motive for murder made the task of the police more than usually difficult and, in spite of some clever deduction and thorough detective work, which led to a possible suspect, it is doubtful if the murderer could ever have been brought to trial without the help of Dr Pereira and her colleagues.

Detective Superintendent John Cummings, in charge of the investigation, built up the following timetable of events of the day of the murder. Just after 5.30 pm, twenty-year-old Mrs Josephs, a petite brunette, left the office where she worked at West Wickham in Kent. She was wearing a blue raincoat over a cerise mini dress. A colleague, Rosemary Scorey, gave her a lift in her car as far as the end of Kingswood Road. By 5.45 pm she was putting her key into the front door of the flat that she and her husband had moved into soon after their return from an Ibiza honeymoon. Five minutes later she telephoned a friend for a brief chat.

At about 6.0 she opened her cookery book to study a recipe for lemon soufflé. Because the central heating was not working and the flat was cold, Mrs Josephs kept her raincoat on while she started preparations for supper, but she changed from her outdoor shoes into a pair of pink slippers. Sometime between 7.0 and 7.30 somebody else entered the flat and killed her – probably with a long-bladed bread-knife with a serrated edge which had been given to the Josephs as a wedding present. It was deduced that she knew her killer because there was no sign of forcible entry to the flat and two used coffee cups and a plate of biscuits were found in the kitchen.

Her twenty-one-year-old husband was home later than usual from the East London office where he worked as a cashier. He and his wife had been invited to the wedding in Wales, later that week, of his boss's son, Mr John Delaney, and on the night of the murder he had joined in a small office party held to celebrate the occasion. It was just after 8.0 pm when he arrived at Deepdene Court and noticed that the whole block was in darkness. The top flat was unoccupied and the Greek couple in the ground-floor flat were out, but he was surprised to see his own first-floor flat also without lights.

As he entered the flat he saw the cookery book, open at the soufflé recipe, lying on the floor. One of his wife's pink slippers was in a corner of the kitchen. He went into the bedroom and found his wife lying in a corner. Her head had been almost severed. She was fully clothed, apart from one slipper, and was still wearing her raincoat over her dress. A roll of banknotes on a table beside the bed had not been touched.

The attack was so savage and so seemingly motiveless that police feared that they might be searching for a homicidal maniac. Detective Superintendent Cummings, speaking on *Independent Television News* the following evening, said: 'It was a senseless killing in every respect. The killer may strike again.'

An intensive hunt was made for the breadknife, the only thing missing from the flat, and neighbours were asked to look in their gardens in case it had been tossed over a hedge or fence by the murderer as he hurried away. A team of Royal Engineers was called in to help in the search for the weapon, and gardens and waste land near Kingswood Road were combed by men with mine detectors. They found two knives, but not the one for which the police were looking. Police dogs also failed to find anything useful.

It was one of those cases in which there was no logical point from which to start inquiries and most of the information given to the police led only to false trails. There was, for instance, the suspicious woodman. Neighbours of the Josephs told the police about a man who touted for business in the area, asking householders if they wanted any trees lopped. They were given a description of this man who, it was said, always called on Wednesdays at the houses and flats in Kingswood Road – and it was on a Wednesday that Claire Josephs was killed. They found the man easily enough – and he proved to be a quite innocent cutter of trees who, in any event, was not in the area on 7 February.

A more promising lead came from a young husband who telephoned the police at Bromley to tell them about a strange man who had called on his wife. He said that soon after his wedding this man telephoned his parents, claiming to be a friend, and asking for their son's new address. He then called on the wife, but she refused to let him in. It seemed possible that this mysterious stranger was following up wedding reports in the local papers with the idea of contacting the brides, either for some perverse reason or because he was a salesman hoping to do business with gullible young housewives.

Claire Josephs, the daughter of Mr and Mrs Roland Parvin, of Wickham Way, Beckenham, had married Bernard Josephs, whose parents lived in near-by Hayes Way, at Christ Church, Beckenham, in September 1967. Two hundred guests had attended the wedding and it was possible that the man the police were told about had read reports of the marriage or had subsequently heard about it from other sources.

Detectives contacted all newly married couples in the Bromley and Beckenham area and appealed, through the press, for information from any newly-weds who had been troubled by strangers calling or telephoning. Again, they draw blank.

The case reported appeared to be an isolated incident and the caller was never traced.

Reverting to their original theory that the killer had been someone known to Mrs Josephs, police officers sifted all her personal papers – and found that she had hoarded birthday and Christmas cards, letters, wedding and party invitations dating back several years. This gave a useful lead to her friends and acquaintances, most of whom, together with the rest of the two hundred guests who had attended the Josephs's wedding, were traced and interviewed.

Among the pile of old invitations was one to the wedding of a girl called Mary, a business colleague of Claire Josephs, to Roger John Payne, in October 1966. When police made a routine call on Payne, a twenty-six-year-old bank clerk, at his home at Ivens Way, Harrietsham, near Maidstone, Kent, his immediate and highly suspicious reaction to their first approach was: 'I am saying nothing without a lawyer.' The officers noticed that he had a cut on his head and injuries to his hands. His name was checked at Scotland Yard's Criminal Records Office and it was found that he had two convictions for assaulting women.

As a suspect he was obviously No. 1, but to confirm these suspicions was an altogether different matter. He had not been seen by anyone who could identify him near the Shortlands flat on 7 February and he had an apparently sound alibi for the time in question. But the proof against him was there waiting to be fed to the 'laboratory detectives'. Margaret Pereira and her colleagues were eventually to present it as incontrovertible evidence of guilt. They established that blood from the groups of the murdered girl and Payne were both on a handkerchief found outside the bedroom door of the flat. Payne's was of a fairly common group, but Mrs Josephs's blood was a variant of the AB group (AB-MN/PGM21), which is shared by not more than one in a hundred people in this country.

The handkerchief was of the same type as those used by Payne, but was a little smaller. Dr Pereira took it apart thread by thread. She found that it was of the same make and material as one taken from Payne's wardrobe but that it had been washed more often and had consequently shrunk. On the bloodstained handkerchief Dr Pereira also discovered a few hairs from Payne's dog.

There was more blood on the suspected man's hat and in the pocket of his Morris car, registration number FDE 937 – all of Mrs Josephs's rare group. Police formed the theory that Payne put the blood-stained knife, which was never found, in the pocket of the car before he dumped the weapon somewhere after driving away from the flat.

Dr Pereira, who is also the Yard's leading textiles expert, matched fibres from Payne's trousers, jacket, overcoat and scarf with fibres found on the blue raincoat Mrs Josephs was wearing when she was killed, and proved that a thin strand of thread found under the dead girl's thumbnail had come from the scarf. Fibres from Claire Josephs's cerise mini dress were embedded in the jacket of Payne's suit, which had been steam-pressed but not cleaned, and more cerise fibres were on the floor of his car. Analysis of the saliva (which can be grouped in the same way as blood) on one of the coffee cups in the kitchen at Deepdene Court revealed that it matched Payne's saliva.

Roger John Payne was arrested and charged with the murder of Claire Josephs. When his trial opened at the Old Bailey on 15 May 1968, before Mr Justice Cooke, the case for the Crown was put by Mr. John Buzzard. Payne was defended by Mr W. Fordham QC.

Mr Buzzard said that the case depended on circumstantial evidence, but that the scientific evidence which connected Payne with the crime was overwhelming. It was an apparently motiveless murder because there was no robbery and no sexual assault. Mrs Josephs had been a friend of Payne's wife and had attended their wedding in 1966, but there was no evidence that Mrs Josephs had met the accused man again until early in January 1968, when he called at the flat to collect his wife. It was the Crown's case that Payne had called again on Claire Josephs during the early evening of 7 February and had been invited in and given coffee and biscuits. Payne had then made a savage attack on the woman, attempting to strangle her before slashing her throat and stabbing her four times. He was a man with a strong sexual urge which could not be satisfied because he was impotent.

When questioned by the police, Payne explained the blood on his hat by saying that the bonnet of his car had fallen on his head. Told that the police intended to interview his wife, he said: 'It is no use seeing her because she cannot say where I was at 7.0 pm.' He had not been given the time of Mrs Josephs's death!

Dr James Malcolm Cameron, Senior Lecturer in Forensic Medicine at the London Hospital Medical School, told the court that the attack on Mrs Josephs was 'maniacal'. There had been an attempt at manual strangulation which would have made her unconscious, but the cause of death was haemorrhage and an air embolism.

Payne, in the witness-box, denied killing Claire Josephs. He said that he had only met her once in his life and was not at her flat on the night of the murder. On that day, 7 February, he had worked at his bank at Maidstone until 11.30 am and then driven to Fleet Street for an interview about another job. He left London at about 3.20 pm and went to Sutton, Surrey, with the idea of visiting a Mr and Mrs Golding. They were not at home, so at about 4.30 pm he decided to call on his mother, who lived at Carshalton, only a mile or two away, but his car broke down. He stopped to repair it, arriving at his mother's home between 6.45 and 7.0 pm. He left Carshalton at 7.40 and started to drive home to Maidstone, but his car broke down again and he eventually arrived home at 9.50.

It was when he was repairing the car for the second time, he continued, that the bonnet fell on his head and blood from the injury stained his hat. His clothes became covered with grease and that was why he had taken them to the cleaners the next day, to have the trousers cleaned and the jacket pressed. Questioned by Mr Buzzard, Payne said that it was not true that he was at his mother's house for only a few minutes, neither was it correct to say that he had subsequently telephoned her to persuade her to alter her story to the police concerning the time he had been with her that evening.

The injuries to his hands had not been inflicted by Mrs Josephs but had been caused by his wife two or three days before the murder. While watching television they had had an argument about their cat. He had pushed his wife and she had scratched and bitten him, taking skin off his fingers and thumbs.

Mr Buzzard cross-examined Payne about the handkerchief found at the flat, the fibres from his suit and from Mrs Josephs's clothing, his saliva on the coffee cup, and the blood mark of the same group as that of the murdered woman in the pocket of his car. 'I can't explain that,' said Payne.

Mr. Buzzard: 'You killed this woman, possibly because she refused your advances. Is this not the truth?'

Payne: 'No, I did not do it. There is only one woman for me in my life and that is my wife.'

The story of the fight over the cat was told to the court by his wife, Mrs Mary Cynthia Payne, twenty-year-old book-keeper, who said that the cat was on her husband's lap and they both wanted it. 'I am afraid I lost my temper and tried to get the cat from him,' she said. 'I lost my balance and fell back on the settee and my ring cut my husband's hand. I got very hysterical and am not really sure what I did. I know I scratched him.'

That incident had occurred on 4 February. When her husband arrived home on 7 February his trousers were muddy and he was wet. He told her that the car had 'played him up'. He had a bruise in the centre of his forehead and a small cut on top of his head and she believed he also had a bruised thumb.

Mr Buzzard: 'Are you by any chance trying to help your husband by saying that your ring scratched his thumb and that he had a similar scratch on the back of his hand?' – 'No.'

Mr Buzzard: 'In fact there were more injuries to his hands after 7 February than there were before?'

Mrs Payne: 'If there were any they were very small. I would not say there were many more, if there were any.'

Mr Kevin Smith, a business colleague of the accused man, said that he remembered scratches on Payne's hands on 6 February. Payne had told him that his wife had caused them during an argument.

The accused man's mother, Mrs Irene Payne, of Peter-borough Road, Carshalton, a shorthand-typist employed at South Western Magistrates' Court, said it was not true that she had given her son a false alibi for the night of the murder.

On 24 May 1968, after a retirement of three and three-quarter hours, the jury found Payne guilty of murder by a majority of eleven to one. Passing sentence of life imprisonment, Mr Justice Cooke told him: 'This was a most brutal and terrible attack.'

Margaret Pereira, whose painstaking work in the laboratory was primarily responsible for proving the killer's guilt, was not in court to hear the verdict, but later that day she had a quite accidental encounter with Bernard Josephs, the husband of the murdered girl. 'Thank you – you've been wonderful,' he said.

The comparatively rare AB blood group was also a factor of considerable significance in a double murder which took place nearly twenty years before the killing of Claire Josephs. The central characters of this tragic case were Leopold Goodman, a forty-nine-year-old Russian Jew, who lived with his wife Esther, aged forty-seven, in a spacious detached house at Ashcombe Gardens, Edgware, in North London; their daughter, Gertrude Marie, a beautiful auburn-haired girl aged twenty; and Gertrude's husband, Daniel Raven, a handsome young man of twenty-three years. The Ravens lived in Edgwarebury Lane, only a short distance from the Goodmans.

The evening of 10 October 1949 began happily for all of them. Four days earlier Marie (as young Mrs Raven was always called) had become the mother of a son, an event of great pride and delight to all the family. At 8.0 pm on 10 October she was visited by her parents at a nursing-home in Muswell Hill, N10. A few minutes later her husband arrived and there was a good deal of excited chat about the weight and welfare and possible name of the baby. The joy of the grandparents was shared by other members of their family and each evening since the birth they had been visited by relatives who were anxious to have the latest news of the child. On 10 October, just before 10.0 pm, Mr Frederick Fraiman, of Marlborough Avenue, Edgware – a brother-in-law of Mrs Goodman – called with his wife and eldest daughter, June, at the house in Ashcombe Gardens. The Fraimans knew that the Goodmans had been going to the nursing-home, as they had done each evening since the birth, and were surprised to get no reply to their knocking because the car in the garage indicated that the couple had returned. After trying both front and side doors they noticed an open window and Mr Fraiman decided to climb in.

In the living-room he was faced with a scene of appalling carnage. Both the Goodmans were dead. The killer had beaten them about the heads with great ferocity, Mr Goodman suffering at least fourteen separate injuries and his wife having been struck seven times.

Detective Chief Superintendent Peter Beveridge, Detective Inspector John Diller and Detective Chief Inspector Albert Tansill all went to the house to investigate what at first looked like a case of murder by an intruder seeking cash and valuables. The weapon of death was obviously the base of a television aerial which was lying in the sink, with blood congealing on it. In a bedroom upstairs they found that the covers had been dragged from the bed. Mrs Goodman's handbag, open and emptied of money, was lying on the floor.

A burglar who had been surprised by the Goodmans? Possibly. But there were several inconsistencies which puzzled the detectives. The window found open by Mr Fraiman had not been broken or forced and, as it opened outwards, could only have been released by someone *inside* the room. Although cash had been taken from the handbag, six £1 notes were still on a bedside table – hardly likely to have been overlooked by a professional thief. It seemed as if Mr Goodman had been sitting at a table when he was first struck because there was a large dent in the middle of the table – indicating that the killer had been standing behind his victim, who had moved his head at the last moment. Mr Goodman's spectacles appeared to have fallen from his nose to the table.

The light in the living-room was not on when Mr Fraiman entered. As it was unlikely that the Goodmans had been sitting in darkness, the killer must have switched off the light before he left. But the switch in the normal place near the door was faulty and disconnected, and the new switch was on the skirting-board behind the door – a peculiarity of the room that could not have been known to a stranger. In a cupboard under the stairs there was a safe containing more than £2,500 in £5, £1 and 10s notes. The detectives were told that the key to this safe was usually kept under the mattress in the

Goodmans' bedroom. This no doubt explained the disorder in the room upstairs – but again implied pre-knowledge on the part of the killer.

It was decided that the young mother in the nursing-home should be spared the news of her parents' death for as long as possible, but a messenger was sent to tell Daniel Raven what had happened.

The young man appeared terribly shocked when he arrived at the Goodmans' house a few minutes later. As he glanced at the body of his mother-in-law he burst into uncontrollable sobs and had to be given a glass of water before he could compose himself enough to talk to the police. 'Why didn't they let me stop? Why did they tell me to go?' he kept asking as he told his story of how he and the Goodmans had arrived at Ashcombe Gardens together after the visit to the nursing-home. He had suggested that he should stay the night because their home had recently been burgled and he didn't like to think of them being alone, but they wouldn't hear of it and he had stayed only for a few minutes before leaving for his own home at about 9.30 pm.

While Raven was talking Inspector Diller was watching him. He noticed that the young man's pale-grey suit was quite uncreased and that he was wearing a clean white shirt. It all looked *too* fresh, thought Diller, and he telephoned the nursing-home to find out what Raven had been wearing when he visited his wife. 'A dark suit,' said a nurse. 'Definitely dark.' Diller hurried to Raven's house – and arrived just in time. A gas poker, still alight, was in the kitchen boiler, and there was a strong smell of burning cloth. Most of the contents of the fire had been destroyed, but the detective was able to salvage a few pieces of a dark jacket and trousers. In the garage he found a pair of blood-stained shoes and saw that there was blood on the steering wheel, driving-seat and handbrake of the car.

Questioned again, Raven changed his story slightly. He said that his parents-in-law had left the nursing-home first and had been in their house a few minutes before he arrived. He asked if he could stay the night because he did not like being in his own home alone, but the Goodmans had refused his request. He had been undressed ready to take a bath when news

161

of the tragedy reached him, so he had put on 'the first clothes to hand' before hurrying to Ashcombe Gardens. He could give no explanation of the clothing in the boiler fire.

The unburned portions of these clothes were sent to Scotland Yard's Forensic Laboratory, together with the shoes from Raven's garage and the television aerial base which had been the weapon of death. Both Mr and Mrs Goodman were of blood group AB, the rarest of the groups, and so, not unexpectedly, was the blood on the aerial. Had the murdered couple been of a more common blood group, the tale told by the other items would not have been so conclusive, but when it was found that all the stains on Raven's clothes and car were also of group AB (not his own blood group) there seemed little doubt that he was the murderer.

Faced with this evidence, Daniel Raven once again changed his story. This time he said that when he arrived at the Goodmans' home he found the front door open and was horrified to find his parents-in-law dead in the living-room. As he bent over to examine them he got blood on his trousers and his shoes. He panicked because he thought he might be suspected of the murder, so hurried home to burn his suit and wash his shoes. It was a feeble story but he stuck to it when he was charged with murder before Mr Justice Cassels at the Old Bailey in November 1949.

His counsel, Mr John Maude, KC, sought to persuade the jury that the crime had been committed by some other person. Goodman was a man who was known to carry large quantities of cash with him and there was also the 'bait' of the money in the safe, so that a dishonest person could have been attracted to the house as 'a good crib to crack'. There was, too, the possibility that it was a crime of revenge because Goodman had assisted the police in some investigations they had been making into currency offences.

After a three-day hearing the jury took fifty minutes to find Daniel Raven guilty of killing Leopold Goodman. A further indictment, charging him with the murder of Esther Goodman, was ordered to remain on the file. His appeal was dismissed in December 1949, and in January the following year the Home Secretary, Mr Chuter Ede, dismissed further appeals for a reprieve which were made on the grounds that he was insane.

The convicted man was hanged on 6 January 1950, for a murder for which the motive remained obscure. There were three theories: one, that Raven hated his parents-in-law because they did not approve of his marriage to their daughter and because Leopold Goodman, after giving him a job as a salesman in his radio components business, dismissed him as 'unsatisfactory' after twelve months; two, that the young husband, heavily in debt and desperate for ready cash, had been trying to rob the Goodmans of the money in the safe when they returned home and caught him; three, that he was in fact insane.

Evidence relating to his mental condition could not be introduced at his trial because he insisted upon his complete innocence, but it was later revealed that he had shown some abnormalities since an air crash of which he was the sole survivor soon after he joined the RAF at the age of sixteen. It can be no more than speculation because, until the last moment of his life, he continued to say, 'I did not do it.'

His tragic young widow, left with a baby son and bereaved of parents and husband within the space of four months, changed her name so as to start a new life. But there was a happy postscript nearly a year later. In December 1950 Marie Raven remarried at a London synagogue; the man's name was kept secret by pressmen who mingled with the two hundred guests at the Savoy Hotel reception.

It is perhaps ironic that the setting for another double murder, which took place in the summer of 1956, should have been within a few hundred yards of a house once occupied by Sir Arthur Conan Doyle, creator of Sherlock Holmes – because it was eventually the Holmesian deduction of Scotland Yard's laboratory team which convicted the killer.

The murder was discovered when a motorist driving through the New Forest, near Cadnam, Hampshire, on Sunday 17 June saw a man leaning over the bonnet of a car parked on the grass verge. As the motorist slowed the man staggered over to him and said, 'Get the police. There's been a murder in the forest, a fight with two women. I've a knife in me.' The man had in fact a four-inch knife wound in the stomach. As he was rushed to hospital at Southampton, PC Roland Jacob went to a part of the forest that the man had described as the murder scene. In a leafy glade in Bignell Wood, Minstead – only a short distance from the busy A31 trunk road – the constable found the remains of a picnic which had ended in death. A small wood fire was still burning, there was tea in an aluminium teapot and warm water in a little tin kettle. Stretched out on the ground was a woman who had been stabbed and bludgeoned and a young girl with stab wounds in the chest and stomach and injuries to her face. Both were dead.

Detective Chief Superintendent Walter Jones, head of Hampshire CID, led the investigating team, which included Chief Inspector L. C. Orchard, from Lymington, and Detective Inspector A. G. Stuchfield, in charge of the New Forest CID. They uncovered a sordid story of love, hate, jealousy – and fatalistic premonition.

The murdered woman was Mrs Lydia Margaretta Leakey, not unattractive at fifty-three, the wife of Thomas Vincent Leakey, a machine operator who had lost one leg in the First World War. The girl was their daughter, fourteen-year-old Norma Noreen, a precociously pretty grammar-school girl. The family lived in Alexandra Road, Parkstone, near Poole, Dorset, where until two weeks before the tragedy they had as a lodger the man who had been taken to hospital with stab wounds – tall, slim and rather handsome Albert William Goozee, thirty-three-year-old ex-merchant seaman who was at that time employed as a labourer.

Goozee had joined the Leakey household in January 1955, occupying the 'best' bedroom while Norma and her mother shared another of the three bedrooms. Mr Leakey slept alone in a small back room. Mrs Leakey, who had not had sexual relations with her husband for some years, was immediately attracted to the lodger – and so apparently was Norma. At the girl's thirteenth birthday party on 4 February 1955, when everyone, including invited children, drank a good deal of cider and cheap red wine, they played a kind of 'postman's knock' game called 'spin the bottle'. Fate, or perhaps a cunning spin of the bottle, decreed that Lydia Leakey and Goozee should go outside the room and kiss, and that was the beginning of a highly charged triangular relationship that was to end only with death.

164

That night Mrs Leakey joined her lodger in his bed and from that date on she spent most nights with him, returning to her own room just before her husband's alarm-clock rang in the mornings. According to Goozee, who was the only one left to tell the tale, Norma sometimes got into bed with them. The three became almost inseparable and enjoyed frequent outings together. Mrs Leakey provided most of the money for a second-hand car for weekend and evening trips and also bought a bicycle for Goozee so that he could accompany Norma on country rides. Tom Leakey was not included in any of these excursions and the situation naturally led to quarrels. Perhaps because Goozee realized that the husband was getting suspicious, or possibly because he himself was becoming weary of the affair, he left the house in December 1955 and signed on for twelve years in the army, asking to be posted as far away from Hampshire as possible.

He was sent to Catterick. But Mrs Leakey wrote to him nearly every day, sending him small sums of money and begging him to return. When he refused she threatened to tell the police that he had had sexual relations with her daughter, still only thirteen years of age. He bought himself out of the army for £30, of which £28 was paid by Mrs Leakey – although Goozee maintained that he had never had intercourse with Norma. The post-mortem examination showed, in fact, that the girl was a virgin.

Goozee went back to Alexandra Road and the sleeping arrangements were resumed on the same basis as before. Lydia Leakey shared the lodger's bed as soon as her husband was in his own room. Norma insisted on joining them, occupying their bed while they made love together, and threatening to tell her father what was going on if she was sent back to the room that she was supposed to be sharing with her mother. At one point Tom Leakey walked out of the house and went to live with relatives in Andover, but he returned after a few weeks and ordered Goozee to go. The lodger departed once more – but again returned after Mrs Leakey had written begging him to do so. She promised to be 'just a mother' to him and signed the letter 'Mum and Norma'.

It was back to square one.

The husband kept telling the lodger to go. The wife said

that if he *did* go she would tell the police about the daughter being in bed with them. The daughter was threatening to tell the husband of the affair between her mother and the lodger, and demanding a place in the lovers' bed as the price of her silence. It is hardly surprising that Norma told some relatives: 'Albert will kill us one day.' Her mother appeared to have had similar fears because after her death police officers found a will she had made 'to be opened in the event of anything happening to me'.

Eventually, in the first week of June 1956, Goozee found other lodgings in Sunnyhill Road, Parkstone, and left the Leakeys' house for the last time. There is again only Goozee's word for what happened subsequently, but he said he agreed to go on a picnic with Mrs Leakey and Norma on 17 June after the woman had sought him out and said she had something she wanted to tell him. Certainly the three of them did go to the New Forest together and begin preparations for a picnic tea.

Goozee's stories of the triangular relationship and of the final scene played out between the three of them varied a good deal from the day he was taken to hospital to the time he stood in the dock at Winchester Assizes, charged with the murder of Norma Leakey, nearly six months later.

A few hours after the murders he said to Detective Constable Stanley Atkinson, who was keeping a vigil beside the injured man's bed: 'I have read about landladies and lodgers, but I never thought it would happen to me. She knew I was seducing her daughter. What could I do? She bought me the car.' Four days later he asked PC Fred Hunt, 'Do I look insane?' He added, 'I will get away with it. It's hate I have in my mind. That's the worst of carrying on with the lodger. It only causes jealousy.'

A week following the tragedy, while he was still in hospital, he spoke to PC Norman Thompson. 'The whole trouble was blackmail,' said Goozee. 'I used to give the girl anything she asked for, records and so on, or else she would go straight to her father . . . give me a razor blade and I'll do myself in right away. Now I have killed, do you know what I would do? Kill again . . . it's so easy, it goes in like butter. I don't think those things should be obtainable. I thought you would have to push hard. I think that is half the trouble' The injured man was referring to the murder weapon, a stiletto-type commando knife with a six-inch blade which was found in the toolbox of Goozee's car – a knife covered in blood which was to tell its own story to the scientists at Scotland Yard's Forensic Laboratory.

But Goozee was not to know about that when he gave his final account of the tragedy as he stood before Mr Justice Havers and a jury of seven men and five women at Winchester in December 1956. He told them that when he and Mrs Leakey and the girl arrived at the picnic spot the woman told her daughter to go and pick bluebells. When Norma had gone the mother started pestering him to return to her. He refused and Mrs Leakey asked him to have sexual intercourse with her for the last time. 'I told her I was absolutely fed up with what she was doing and I was not enjoying having intercourse with a woman old enough to be my mother,' continued Goozee. 'She promised me that if I would give in to her it would never happen again. With that we started to kiss each other. The check rug was spread beside the car and we both lay down on it. Next I knew Norma was standing beside us. She began calling her mother a dirty rotten beast and said, " Why don't you leave Albert alone?"'

He said that the next thing he knew was that Norma was hitting her mother on the head with an axe they had taken with them to chop wood for the picnic fire. 'The girl then began to scream her head off. She was very hysterical and kept saying, "What have I done? I am very sorry, but Mummy made me do it." I hit her several times across the face with the back of my hand.'

While he was attending to Mrs Leakey, who was bleeding about the head, he pointed out that the police would have to be told the whole story. She had the stiletto knife in her hand and 'went like a mad woman'. He felt the knife go into his stomach. Norma then got between him and her mother and he saw Mrs Leakey lunge at the girl.

Cross-examined by Mr. N. R. Fox-Andrews QC, prosecuting, Goozee said he could not say whether Mrs Leakey stabbed Norma intentionally or by accident. He did not push the knife into Mrs Leakey's stomach. The whole thing was accidental.

Earlier in the hearing, when Goozee was shown the knife with which he was alleged to have stabbed the girl, he said he saw it first during a quarrel with Mrs Leakey when she wanted to send Norma to boarding-school to get her out of the way. On that occasion he saw Mrs Leakey lunge at Norma and he took the knife away from her. He kept it under the driving seat of the car. 'What you meant to do was to finish this ghastly three-sided story by killing the women and then killing yourself, wasn't it?' asked Mr Fox-Andrews.

'I did not,' replied Goozee.

But the blood on the knife told the true story. When it was examined by Dr Lewis Nickolls, then director of the Yard's Forensic Laboratory, it was shown to have blood of two groups on the slender blade. Most of the blood was of group O, matching samples taken from Goozee. Both Mrs Leakey and Norma were of group A, but the only blood of this group was on a small section of the blade close to the handle. It was clear from this evidence that Goozee had been stabbed after the knife had been used on the women. Had his story of the woman's attack on her daughter been true, the A group blood of the girl would have pushed his own O group blood up to the handle of the blade.

Albert Goozee was sentenced to death. His appeal against conviction was dismissed, but he was later reprieved and his sentence commuted to one of life imprisonment.

When the 12.24 pm train from Aldershot, Hampshire, to Waterloo, pulled into the small country station of Ash Vale, Surrey, on 7 April 1965, an off-duty train driver, Mr Ivor Laws, noticed that one of the carriage doors on the offside was swinging open. Railmen searched the train and in one compartment found a woman's handbag, a cream holdall and one high-heeled shoe. Immediately the track was closed to further traffic and the Aldershot stationmaster, Mr Richard Powell, took a special train up the line from Aldershot, which is only five minutes by rail from Ash Vale.

Lying between the tracks, about six hundred yards from Ash Vale, was a badly injured woman. She was still alive, but not sufficiently conscious to speak. Mr Powell tried to save her with the 'kiss of life' but she was dead by the time she arrived at Cambridge Military Hospital, Aldershot. It was at first assumed that she had fallen from the train – until pathologist Dr Keith Mant found that, in addition to having a broken wrist, broken leg and severe head injuries, the woman had nine stab wounds in her chest and eight similar wounds in her back.

Detective Superintendent Edward Hughes, railway police CID chief, joined Detective Chief Superintendent John Place, head of Surrey CID, Detective Chief Inspector Owen Breach, head of Farnham CID, and Detective Chief Superintendent Walter Jones, Hampshire CID chief, to form a formidable murder team.

The victim was Mrs Enid Mary Wheeler, aged thirty-one, who lived with her husband Derek, an instrument maker, in a neat white bungalow in Fir Acre Road, a private road in Ash Vale. A small, pleasant-looking woman with a ready smile, Mrs Wheeler led a quiet life, busy in her home and garden and working part-time as a clerk at Boots the chemists in Aldershot. She had been on her way home from work when she was killed. There seemed no motive for her murder. She had not been sexually assaulted and nothing had been taken from her handbag.

There were only seven passengers in the train between Aldershot and Ash Vale and three of them were in the coach in which the dead woman's possessions were found. One of the three, a twenty-one-year-old labourer, Patrick John Jenner, of Downshill Cottage, Runfold, Surrey, had given his name to the guard at Ash Vale after the open door had been noticed. He told the guard that the articles in the compartment belonged to a woman who had got into the train at Aldershot. He thought there was a man with her. He had no idea what had happened to her but thought he had heard a door banging.

Jenner had stayed on the train until Frimley, the next station up the line. He had then taken a bus back to Aldershot, where he went into the police station and asked what had happened to the woman missing from the train. Chief Inspector Breach told him that her body had been found on the line and that she appeared to have been stabbed to death. Jenner seemed very upset and said, 'Oh good God, is she dead?'

Breach asked if he could throw any light on her death, to which Jenner replied, 'Not me. I haven't the guts to kill a cat.'

It was noticed that the palm of Jenner's right hand was cut and that there were scratch marks on the back of the same hand. The young man explained these injuries by saying that he had fallen over as he alighted from the train at Frimley and had cut his hand on the gravel. But there was no gravel at Frimley station. The platform had a smooth asphalt surface.

Jenner was charged with the murder of Enid Wheeler. At Surrey Assizes three months later Mr Petre Crowder QC, for the Crown, demonstrated how the hilt of the knife used to stab the woman could have inflicted the wound on the accused man's hand. Mrs Wheeler had defence-type cuts on her right hand, consistent with her having gripped the knife.

Other evidence had been found which pointed to him being the killer. A white-handled sheath knife, similar to one Jenner had owned, was found in a wood near the railway line. A tie clip like one that had been given to Jenner as a Christmas present was on the railway line near the body. His palm-print was on the door which had been swinging open. On his cardigan there were some fibres that could have come from the dead woman's coat.

All these clues added up to the strong suspicion that Jenner had killed Enid Wheeler, but none was positive. The one piece of evidence that could not be explained away was the blood on his shoes and his jacket and trousers. Some of it was blood of his own group, but many of the stains were of group A – the same as Mrs Wheeler's blood and of a different group to his own. Jenner's only explanation for the blood on his clothing was that it had come from his injured hand. He could give no reason why group A blood should have been found.

On 8 July 1965, after a three-day hearing, the jury took only twenty-eight minutes to find him guilty of what Mr Justice Fenton Atkinson described as 'a singularly vicious and horrible crime'. Patrick John Jenner was jailed for life for murder without anyone knowing why he had committed the crime.

10

Evidence so rare

Professor John Glaister, formerly Director of Forensic Medicine at Glasgow University, has a theory which he calls 'the key of interchange'. He believes that no crime can be committed without the criminal leaving some sort of 'visiting card' behind and, conversely, that no criminal can avoid taking with him some evidence from the scene of his crime.

Newspaper readers of murder-trial reports are familiar with most of these linking clues. There is the hair from the victim's head on the coat of the killer and fragments of wool from the murderer's sweater under the finger nails of the dead person; the bullet in the heart which matches the gun belonging to the suspected man; substances on the clothes of both attacker and victim identical with substances at the scene of the crime; and a whole Aladdin's cave of evidence which has been revealed by the turning down of trousers turn-ups. Like fingerprints and bloodstains, these are forensic clues familiar to all students of murder, but just occasionally a killer is caught by something quite different. . . .

In the 1958 murder case of prostitute Margaret Brindley, the 'visiting card' – it was described in those words by prosecuting counsel at the subsequent trial of her killer – was a lipstick-stained handkerchief.

Margaret, aged twenty, was one of the nine children of Mr Harold Brindley and his wife, also called Margaret, of Granville Street, Wolverhampton, Staffordshire, but when she was eighteen she left her home and local job at the Ever-Ready factory for what she hoped was to be a more exciting life in London. At first she worked as a waitress in a club, but ten months before she died she met a man who persuaded her to go on the streets – to their mutual financial benefit. Earning about £60 a week, Margaret enjoyed luxuries she had never known before, while her boss, who was also her lover, bought expensive clothes, a flashy car and a half-share in a café. They were able to afford two flats in Islington. The days of wine and roses, however, were very quickly over. Margaret became pregnant and by the end of November 1958 was expecting her baby within a few weeks. Her West End clients were no longer so interested in her services and money began to run short.

On Wednesday, 3 December, a lorry-driver called Robert Long, of Hudson Street, Bicester, Oxfordshire, stopped at a bridge over the River Ray, near the A41 road between Aylesbury and Bicester. The radiator of the lorry had boiled up and he went down the bank to the river to fill a tin with water. There, in rushes underneath the bridge, he found the body of Margaret Brindley.

It was at first impossible to identify her because, in addition to head injuries, her face had been savagely battered, obviously with the intention of making identification difficult. But Detective Superintendent William Baker, of the Murder Squad, had a hunch – and checked the dead woman's fingerprints with those of prostitutes in Scotland Yard's Criminal Records Office. One set matched those of Margaret Brindley, who had been arrested for soliciting in Hyde Park only a few days before.

It was a short step from that to the questioning of the man with whom she had been living, a twenty-one-year-old Turkish Cypriot named Eyyup Celal, who had come to London from Nicosia in October 1957. He told the police that on 30 November he had taken Margaret to Paddington Station so that she could go to her parents in Wolverhampton until after the birth of the baby, and had not seen her since. He had bought a new car, a salmon pink and ivory Vauxhall Cresta, in the middle of November and had never driven it out of London, he added. He declared that on 2 December, the day it was believed that Margaret had been murdered, he had spent the whole day with a girl named Dorothy Johnson. Celal insisted that he had no idea that Margaret Brindley was a prostitute.

His story very quickly collapsed.

Red-haired Dorothy Johnson, another prostitute, said that she had not spent all day with Celal on 2 December. She had spent the night of 1–2 December with him and they kissed before he left her in the morning. Some of her lipstick smudged on to his face and he wiped it off with his monogrammed handkerchief. Evidence that Margaret had been in London after 30 November – the day Celal said he had taken her to Paddington – was given to the police by a girl called Maureen Kelly. She said that on the night of 1 December she and Margaret were together in Hyde Park. According to his usual custom, Celal had driven through the park at about 9.30 pm and had waved to them. She and Margaret parted in Park Lane at about midnight. On Wednesday 3 December she (Maureen Kelly) had asked Celal where Margaret had gone and he told her that he thought she had gone to Birmingham.

Celal's assertion that he had only driven his new car in London during the eighteen days he had owned it became a matter of some doubt when police established that he had travelled more than a thousand miles since taking delivery. An appeal for any witnesses who might have seen a pink and ivory Cresta on the seventeen-mile stretch of road between Bicester and Aylesbury on 2 December – brought responses from a number of people. Among them was a male nurse, Mr Ronald Parrish, of Hulcott, Buckinghamshire. He told detectives that such a car, driven by a man he later identified as Celal, had forced him to pull up sharply on his bicycle at an Aylesbury roundabout at 7.15 pm on 2 December. The Cypriot was also identified by garage attendant Mr Frank Pattenden, who said that on 1 December the man had driven into his garage at Wendover, bought one gallon of petrol and had asked the route to London.

Police formed the theory that Celal had first reconnoitred the area with the idea of finding a suitable place to murder, and to dispose of the body, and on the following day had returned with Margaret Brindley – on the pretext of driving her to Wolverhampton – and had then killed her and mutilated her face so that she could not be recognized. Although Celal had washed the car, including the boot, it still gave a positive result to tests for human blood.

All these circumstances were suspicious, but the proof of Celal's guilt was in two items found at the scene of the murder. One was a hollow metal bar which proved to be part of the steering column of a car. In a garage used by the suspected man police officers discovered a vice which bore marks corresponding to one-thousandth of an inch with marks on the bar. Tiny traces of green paint on the bar were the same as green paint on the door of the house where Celal lived, and inside the bar there were blood spots of Margaret Brindley's blood-group. The second item, the 'visiting card' evidence, was a man's white handkerchief, bearing the initial T, found a few feet from the body. Eyyup Celal was known as 'Tony the Turk' and the same T, in maroon silk, was on all his handkerchiefs and some of his pyjamas and underwear.

As Margaret and the Cypriot had been living together there was no reason why she should not have been carrying one of his handkerchiefs. But there was lipstick on this handkerchief and it was established at the Metropolitan Police Laboratory that it was of the same type as that used by Dorothy Johnson. The constituents of lipstick vary from one manufacturer to another and it is sometimes possible to make a positive identification. In this case it was proved that none of Margaret Brindley's lipsticks were of the same make or shade as that on the handkerchief. It was plain that Celal had been with Margaret after leaving Dorothy on the morning of 2 December.

Twenty-two-year-old Miss Johnson also told detectives that some time early in December Celal had offered her a black and white checked skirt, which she later discovered had belonged to Margaret, and had asked her if she could find any use for some baby's nappies.

The dead girl's body was fully clothed when found, but her handbag was missing. When Celal, charged with her murder, appeared at the Old Bailey in February 1959, a handbag found at his Barnsbury Road flat in Islington was passed to him. 'Can you explain how this was found by the police at Barnsbury Road?' asked Mr George Baker, QC, prosecuting. 'I can't', replied Celal. Mr Baker: 'You appreciate she had no handbag with her when the body was found?' – 'I do not know. I do not know where the body was.'

'You took that handbag back to Barnsbury Road from Bicester, didn't you? – 'I did not go to Bicester.'

When Mr Baker insisted that Celal had taken the handbag, the accused man retorted: 'Go ahead and prove it.'

In reply to further questions, Celal said he had never been

to Hyde Park looking for Margaret and it was a lie to suggest that she had handed him money in the park. He did not know she was a prostitute. 'What did you think she was doing in the evenings?' asked Mr Baker. Celal replied: 'Sometimes she would go out with me and sometimes with her girlfriends.'

The Crown's case was that Margaret was killed by Celal because she had become pregnant and he considered that she was of no further use to him. In whatever direction one looked, said Mr Baker, all the evidence pointed towards Celal. The final link in the chain of circumstantial evidence was the initialled handkerchief and that was 'just like leaving his visiting card'.

A verdict of guilty was returned by the jury after a retirement of fifty-five minutes. Sentencing Celal to life imprisonment, Mr Justice Donovan said to him: 'The jury has pierced the network of lies by which you hoped to confound justice and escape the consequences of this dreadful deed.'

Less than two years later another chapter of the Brindley story was written, a chapter which, had it appeared in a novel, would have been criticized as being 'too far-fetched' – but a chapter which very clearly bears out the old adage that truth really is stranger than fiction.

On 15 August 1960 a woman was found battered to death in a ground-floor bed-sitting-room at Dunstall Hill Road, Wolverhampton – and the woman was Mrs Margaret Brindley, mother of the Margaret Brindley who was killed by Eyyup Celal in December 1958. Because of the extraordinary coincidence, detectives went to Brixton Jail, London, to interview Celal to see if he could give them some clue to murder No. 2, but it was soon clear that the two crimes were quite unconnected. Very little investigation, in fact, was needed to lead the police to the killer of auburn-haired, forty-eight-year-old Mrs Brindley. She had left her husband and was living with a Jamaican in a house which also sheltered a number of other West Indians. Two weeks after the murder one of these men, forty-five-year-old Eric Thomas Nicholson, admitted that he had killed Mrs Brindley in a fit of temper. He had lost his job and as he wanted to send money to his wife and six children in Jamaica, had asked Mrs Brindley if she would repay £5 which she owed him. She replied: 'I don't have time now to talk to any black bastard.' Nicholson flew into a rage and hit her with a shoe he was cleaning.

At Staffordshire Assizes on 2 December 1960 Nicholson was found guilty of non-capital murder and was sentenced to life imprisonment. Harold Brindley was left to mourn both wife and daughter, who lie buried in the same grave in the little parish churchyard of Bushbury, near Wolverhampton. He told reporters: 'I thought I had had all I could stand last time. My wife left me about that time. This is just too much for one person. . . .'

The fact that there were only two specimens of *Sorbus intermedia*, the Swedish whitebeam, in the city of Leicester in 1957 was doubtless a matter of interest only to botanists and their ilk – until the autumn of that year, when leaves from this comparatively rare tree helped to trap a killer.

The murder hunt began when Mr Bert Greet, a factory foreman, of Hand Avenue, Braunstone, Leicestershire, travelling on the top deck of a bus on his way to work early in the morning of 18 September 1957, saw a woman lying on the ground behind the still-locked gates of Grasmere Park. He called the police, who found that the woman – an attractive blonde, wearing a blue and white dress under a raincoat – had been strangled. Detectives at first thought that she was Mrs Margaret Quesada, the British-born wife of a US airman, and called in the Special Investigation Branch of the US Air Force from Molesworth. They established that Mrs Quesada was with her husband in Jacksonville, Kansas. Further inquiries revealed that the murdered woman was Mrs Quesada's sister, twenty-nine-year-old divorcee Mrs Joyce Stanton.

Her open-toed, high-heeled shoes were missing and were later found in the road not far from her one-room flatlet in West Street, about four hundred yards from Grasmere Park.

Detectives, led by Superintendent Eric Lacy, then head of Leicester City CID, checked Mrs Stanton's movements on the previous day, a Tuesday. She had called on a dressmaker in the afternoon and had then visited her parents, Mr and Mrs Alfred Lay, in Outram Street, Leicester. She returned to her flatlet early in the evening and stayed there until 8.30, when a man called for her and they went out together. After a few minutes she returned for her grey raincoat – and was not seen alive again. Police formed the theory that she had been killed at about midnight in a house near the park and that her body had been carried there and dumped by the murderer. There was no sign of any sexual assault.

She was known to have been friendly with a number of Indians and five of them were taken to the police station for questioning. One, a Sikh labourer named Darshan Singh, had been living with Mrs Stanton for some years and was the father of her two illegitimate children. The couple had parted company after the birth of the second child a month before the murder, and it was known that Mrs Stanton had obtained an affiliation order against Singh in respect of this child. Singh was closely questioned, but said that he had not seen Joyce Stanton for several weeks and denied having been in Grasmere Park on 17 September. But when detectives searched his room at Napier Street, Leicester, they found on the floor two bright green leaves with undersides of woolly grey. Examined by botanical experts, these leaves proved to have come from the redberried Swedish white-beam – of which one of Leicester's only two specimens grew in Grasmere Park. The other tree was situated about a mile away.

When twenty-eight-year-old Darshan Singh was tried for murder at Nottingham Assizes on 19 November 1957, Mr W. A. Fearnley-Whittingstall, for the Crown, said that small pieces of grass found in Singh's trouser turn-ups formed another link in 'an unbroken chain of circumstantial evidence'. These grass fragments were similar to samples taken from the site at which the body was found.

The prosecution's case was that the Sikh was infuriated by the bastardy order and had strangled Mrs Stanton, carrying her body to the park in a blanket. Darshan Singh continued to deny any knowledge of the killing, but was found guilty and sentenced to life imprisonment. His application for leave to appeal was refused.

Professor Glaister proved his interchange theory in one murder case which at first seemed entirely without clues to the killer.

One evening in September 1947, a young Scotsman named

Archie McIntyre arrived home from his work as a shepherd and was mildly surprised to find that his mother, Mrs Catherine McIntyre, was apparently not at home. The door of their hill-top cottage, The Towers, Kenmore, near Aberfeldy, Perthshire, was locked, although their cairn terrier was running about the garden. The morning newspapers were still in the letter-box. Archie was not seriously worried until a neighbour arrived to ask what had happened to Mrs McIntyre, who had failed to visit his, the neighbour's, wife, as she had arranged, earlier that afternoon. The young man was afraid that his mother had been taken ill, so he fetched a ladder and climbed into the house through an open upstairs window.

Catherine McIntyre, the forty-seven-year-old wife of a head shepherd and mother of three children, was in one of the bedrooms. Her wrists were tied together with bootlaces, a scarf had been used as a gag, and she had been killed by violent blows about the head. Her wedding ring was missing – and so was a bag containing £90 in notes, money which had been sent by her husband's employer to pay shepherds' wages.

Fingerprint experts closely examined the cottage and all contents, but failed to find a single print that could not be identified. They were forced to conclude that the killer had worn gloves. There was nothing, not one tiny clue, to give the police a lead.

Then Archie McIntyre remembered something. That morning, on his way to work at 8.0 am, he thought he had seen a man's head bobbing about among the trees some distance from the path, about four hundred yards from the cottage. He told the police and was able to take them to the exact spot. Among the thick bracken there was an area of a few yards which had been trampled quite flat and had clearly been used as a hiding-place for the murderer while he watched the comings and goings at the cottage. In what amounted to a lair they found some clothing, a blood-stained handkerchief, part of a sawn-off shotgun and a rusty razor blade, plus the return half of a railway ticket from Aberfeldy to Perth – a special kind of ticket issued only to members of the Forces.

A description of the gun was circulated. It was seen by Mr William Chubb, a farmer of Old Meldrum, Aberdeenshire, about a hundred miles away from the scene of the murder.

Mr Chubb told detectives that he was sure it was one he had borrowed from a neighbour. He had missed it after a man he had employed casually on his farm had left to seek work further south. This man, a Polish soldier named Stanislaw Myszka, had previously been living at a resettlement camp at Taymouth Castle, near Lock Tay, only a few miles from Kenmore, so it seemed possible that he might have known of the arrangement for paying wages to the shepherds of that district. It was all rather nebulous. But it was a start.

Myszka, aged twenty-three and married to a French girl who was still living in Paris, had moved on to Ardallie, in the Buchan district of Aberdeenshire, after leaving the Chubbs. There he had stayed with a Polish couple named Szewe. When he left them on 22 September 1947 he had very few possessions and only a few shillings in his pocket. He returned to the Szewes late at night on 26 September, the day of the murder. He seemed to have acquired plenty of money. Mrs Szewe went into the neighbouring town of Peterhead with him on 27 September, when he bought a suit and shirt for himself and a dress as a present for her. She noticed that he took the money from a wad of £5 notes.

Then a taxi-driver came forward to say that a Pole had hired his cab for the journey from Aberfeldy to Perth on the afternoon of 26 September. His description of the man – slim, shortish, sallow, pointed chin – fitted that of Myszka and the driver also noticed that his fare was wearing brown leather gloves and was carrying a dispatch case. The handkerchief that had been found with the gun and other items in the hideout near the murder cottage was identified by Mrs Isabella Chubb as one she had given to Myszka when he left her husband's farm.

The Szewes, already suspicious of their friend's new-found wealth, were even more concerned when the taxi-driver's description of his passenger was published and it was stated that the police wished to interview the man. Myszka took fright and disappeared. On 2 October 1947 he was found in an old RAF camp near Peterhead and was arrested and charged with murder. In the routine search of his clothing a wedding ring very like the one missing from Mrs McIntyre's finger was found hidden beneath the insole of one of his shoes.

179

There were plenty of clues to link him with the murder, though none was in itself conclusive, and it was left to professor Glaister to provide the clinching evidence when Stanislaw Myszka stood trial at Perth in January 1948.

The razor blade found with the gun and handkerchief had been sent to the professor at Glasgow University. It had been used for a dry shave. A few tiny fair hairs were still clinging to it. These were put under the comparison microscope, alongside some hairs extracted from a razor with which the accused man had been shaved while in prison awaiting trial. The two sets of hairs appeared to be identical.

Professor Glaister, whose book *Hairs of Mammalia* is a standard work of reference for pathologists, was closely questioned by defence counsel, Mr F. C. Watt, and the trial judge, Lord Sorn. Referring to the hair on the first blade, Mr Watt asked the professor if he could exclude absolutely the possibility of these hairs being from the face of some other person. 'We can never say that hair comes from the individual unless we take it from the individual,' replied Professor Glaister.

'You would not go so far as to say that you might not find two identical hairs microscopically from different heads?" asked the judge.

'I can only say that by matching one sample with another, finding the detailed and gross microscopic characters to be identical, it permits us to say that they are consistent with a common source,' answered the witness. In this instance the two sets of hairs he examined were so consistent.

Myszka's defence was that it was a case of mistaken identity, but the jury did not think so. The weight of a few hairs tipped the balance of evidence against him. He was hanged at Perth Jail on 6 February 1948.

Hairs of a different kind, those of the humble British wild rabbit, played a significant part in the conviction of another murderer. As in the Myszka case, alone they would have meant nothing, but they were the one unusual feature among otherwise commonplace evidence. Although it was eventually his own incredible stupidity that sent this killer to the gallows in the dark, wartime days of 1944, it is doubtful if he would have been arrested in the first place had it not been for the skill of the forensic scientists – and those rabbit hairs among some dust in a ditch.

The victim of the murder for which he was hanged was Winifred Mary Evans, a twenty-seven-year-old WAAF wireless operator stationed at a RAF aerodrome near Beccles, Suffolk. It was a murder of lust – she had been raped and suffocated. The crime could have been committed by any of the hundreds of RAF personnel at the camp, or by any of two hundred Italians at a nearby prisoner-of-war camp, or by one of the American servicemen stationed at a base ten miles away – or, in fact, by any man who might have been near the scene of the killing on that black, cold night of 8–9 November 1944. It was the back-room boys of the police force who found the evidence which pointed to one particular British airman – and the man himself who later provided the clinching proof of his guilt.

Winnie Evans, unlike many victims of sexual violence, was a girl of high moral character. She had certain standards by which she stood firm and, even in the atmosphere of moral laxity engendered by wartime conditions, refused to weaken. She was an attractive girl, with light-brown, wavy hair and unusually beautiful eyes. A very good dancer, she was never short of boyfriends, but those who tried to become too familiar with her were smartly put in their places. To Winnie, sex was something which came after, not before, marriage. She had not been long at the Beccles camp, but long enough for any over-fresh young airman to discover that a stinging slap round the face was likely to be her response to suggestions of conduct she considered out of place. She had not been keen to join the WAAF, but in those days of conscription for women as well as men she had the choice of working in a factory or going into the Services, and she picked the job for which she thought she was best suited.

In the fateful way in which tragedy seems to pursue some families, the Evans had already suffered more than their share. One of Winnie's twin brothers had been killed in Libya, her father had died – it is said of a broken heart – shortly afterwards, and her mother survived this double loss for only a few years. Winnie, left without parents, went to live with her married sister, a Mrs Roberts, at 'Rockhurst', Acton Lane,

Harlesden, in North-West London. It was from there that she went first to Portsmouth and later to Beccles for service in the WAAF.

On the evening of 8 November 1944, Winnie Evans and her friend, WAAF Corporal Margaret Elizabeth Johns, joined a number of others from the camp at a dance at the American base near Norwich and they all came back by lorry, arriving just before midnight. Winnie was due on duty at midnight, so quickly went into her hut to change from her dancing clothes into uniform. Margaret asked Winnie if she should accompany her part of the way to the signals office, but Winnie replied gaily: 'No, I shall be all right.' She took her bicycle lamp and walked briskly down the lane.

Corporal Johns went into the women's washing-shed and was startled to see a man in RAF uniform crouching against a wall in one of the cubicles. She asked him what he was doing there and he replied: 'I am lost. Is this No. I site?' Margaret Johns told him sharply that he was in the WAAF section and ordered him to get out, but he pleaded; 'Will you show me the way out? I am drunk and can't see.'

Realizing that he was, in fact, drunk – he was falling about by this time – Margaret told him which way to go. The airman came towards her and asked: 'Can I thank you?' Margaret retorted: 'No, you cannot. Get down the road.' She saw him off the site and watched him go along the lane down which Winnie Evans had walked only about ten minutes earlier. It was 12.30 am when Corporal Johns eventually went into her own hut to go to bed.

Soon after 7.30 the next morning a forty-five-year-old electrician's mate, Claude Fiske, cycling from his home at Darby Road, Beccles, to work on the Nissen huts at the RAF camp, saw a WAAF greatcoat in a ditch under some overhanging hawthorn brambles. He got off his bicycle with the idea of picking up the coat and handing it in at the camp, but as he stepped forward he saw the legs of a girl protruding from the coat. She was lying on her stomach and had obviously been the victim of an assault.

Fortunately for the police, Fiske was a thriller fan with a great interest in murder and one of the lessons he had learned was never to touch anything at the scene of a crime. He went straight to the RAF guardroom and told the duty officer to phone the police. Within twenty-four hours Detective Chief Inspector (later Detective Chief Superintendent) Ted Greeno, with Detective Sergeant Fred Hodge and Home Office pathologist Keith Simpson, arrived at Beccles from Scotland Yard, and a full-scale murder hunt was launched.

It was not long before Inspector Greeno heard about Corporal Johns's midnight encounter with the mysterious airman and it was obvious that this man had to be found. Greeno suspected, however, that an immediate line-up of all local RAF men, for purposes of identification, might panic the one they wanted into destroying available evidence, so he waited for the Friday pay parade and discreetly positioned Margaret Johns in such a way that she could see but not be seen. Without any hesitation she picked out Leading Aircraftman Arthur Heys, a thirty-seven-year-old married man with three children, of Harold Street, Colne, Lancashire.

When questioned, Heys admitted that he was the man who had been seen by Corporal Johns in the women's washroom and said he had missed his way after having been on a pub crawl in Beccles. Upon receiving instructions from Corporal Johns, he added, he had gone straight to his quarters, arriving at 12.30 am. Other airmen in his hut, however, told the police that Heys had not appeared until between 1.0 and 1.30 am. His shoes were muddy and his uniform was stained and also covered in mud. He had missed breakfast the following morning and had spent the time cleaning his uniform.

All his clothing was sent away for scientific examination and the following evidence was found: there were rabbit hairs on his trousers which matched those on the girl's torn clothing; gritty brick dust, of a kind which, in that area, existed only in the ditch in which the dead girl was found, was on Heys's shoes; one hair which *could* have come from Winnie Evans's head was embedded in the fabric of his tunic; bloodstains on the tunic were of the same group as the girl's blood.

Superintendent Greeno, when interviewing Heys, noticed two large fresh scratches on the airman's hand. A war reserve policeman, Matthew Robert Mason, told Greeno that Heys had called at Beccles police station at 11.0 pm on 8 November – only about an hour before the murder – to report that his bicycle had been lost or stolen, and at that time there were no marks on his hand. Mason said that Heys appeared to be sober, although he smelled of alcohol.

Heys was arrested and charged with murder and remanded to Norwich Jail. Even so, the evidence against him was all circumstantial and it is by no means certain that a jury would have convicted him without some corroboration. Heys had admitted that he was drunk that night – the war reserve constable agreed that he had been drinking – and a jury might have thought it possible that he had staggered into the ditch and accidentally picked up the damning dust and rabbit hairs.

Then on 9 January 1945, a day before the final hearing at Beccles Magistrates' Court, an anonymous letter arrived at the RAF camp, addressed to the Officer Commanding, Air Sea Rescue Squadron, Beccles, Suffolk. Written in block letters with a blue pencil, it read: 'Will you please give this letter to solicitors for the airman so wrongly accused of murdering Winnie Evans. I want to state that I am the person responsible for the above mentioned girl's death. I had arranged to meet her at the bottom of the road where the body was found, at midnight. When I arrived she was not there. I waited some time and decided to walk down towards the WAAF quarters. Just before I reached this I heard a voice and stood close to the hedge. I heard footsteps. It proved to be an airman. I don't think he saw me. I then saw the dark figure of someone else coming in the same direction. As she got near I recognized it was Winnie and I spoke to her and we proceeded together towards the road. She said I should not have come down there to meet her. A WAAF friend had offered to go along with her as the airman ahead was drunk and had lost his way.

'She had her cycle lamp with her. No one will ever find this. She told me she could not stay long being nearly half-past twelve. She should have been on duty. She accepted money from me which I got back, finding she was unclean. This is the type of girl she was, a gold digger. I have known her to go with three Yanks in one night. I must have gone mad. I don't remember exactly what happened. I know we struggled and I tore her tunic and slacks and I believe other things and I was most indecent. Since then I have covered up my tracks and got rid of all my clothing which were covered with blood down the front.'

The letter ended by saying that the writer would shortly be going overseas and asked that his 'humble apologies' be conveyed to the airman concerned. Greeno was immediately suspicious of this letter and was convinced that Heys had written it himself and somehow succeeded in smuggling it out of prison for posting. The damning phrase, of course, was 'the airman ahead was drunk and had lost his way'. Only Heys and Corporal Johns knew of the washroom incident. Winnie Evans knew nothing about this lost airman because she had parted from Corporal Johns *before* the man was found in the washing-shed.

The letter had certainly been written by an airman because to the general public the Beccles camp was known to be occupied simply by No. 3 Squadron RAF. The fact that it was an air-sea rescue base was known only to squadron members and RAF officials. Equally certainly the letter had been written by the killer of Winnie Evans. Nobody but the murderer and Corporal Johns knew of the existence of the bicycle lamp. The reference to the girl being 'unclean' meant that she was menstruating at the time – a fact known only to the detectives, the doctors and the man who killed her. The letter-writer was lying about Winnie's morals because the pathologist had established that she was *virgo intacta* until she was raped and killed.

Detective Superintendent Fred Cherrill, who was a handwriting expert as well as Scotland Yard's top fingerprint man at that time, was given the task of deciding whether or not Arthur Heys was the writer of the anonymous letter – and he decided that he was. At Norwich Jail he found blue crayon pencils similar to the one used by the writer and discovered that it would have been quite simple for Heys to have given the letter to any one of thirty prisoners who daily left the jail for work outside. Cherrill compared the letter to the writing on the forms on which Heys had applied for leave and also to some block-letter writing on a tab attached to a watch that Heys was repairing for a friend. In each case he found a number of similarities – enough for him to be sure that they had all been written by the same person.

185

Evidence on his findings was given by Cherrill when Heys was tried for murder before Mr Justice MacNaghten at Suffolk Assizes, Bury St Edmunds, in January 1945. Mr John Flowers KC, for the Crown, asked Cherrill: 'What is your opinion as to whether the anonymous letter was or was not written by the same person who printed the letters on the leave forms and the watch tab?' Cherrill replied: 'It was the same person.'

'Have you any doubts about it at all?' – 'No.'

'If the other ones were written by the prisoner, so was the anonymous letter?' – 'Yes.'

Mr Flowers drew the jury's attention to the passage in the letter which mentioned an airman who had lost his way. 'Nobody in the world could have put this in the letter except Heys,' he said. 'There was only one man drunk and lost and that was the prisoner.'

Heys, defended by Mr F. T. Alpe, admitted that on returning from Beccles on the night of the murder he had strayed into the WAAF washing-hut by mistake and that Corporal Margaret Johns had found him and sent him on his way. He denied, however, that he had subsequently caught up with Winnie Evans and said that he had not even seen her. When Mr Alpe asked him: 'Did you kill Winnie Evans?' Heys replied firmly, 'No, I did not.' He was equally emphatic in his denial of authorship of the anonymous letter. Asked by Mr Flowers to explain the blood on his tunic – of the same group as Winnie Evans's blood and of a different group to his own – Heys said that he had helped a man who had cut his hand when falling from a bicycle.

The jury was out for only forty minutes, at the end of the three-day hearing, before returning a verdict of guilty. Passing the death sentence, Mr Justice MacNaghten described the crime as 'savage and horrible'. Heys protested, 'God knows I am innocent of this foul crime. I know God will look after me. I am not afraid.'

Reference to 'the fatal anonymous letter was again made on 26 February 1945, when Heys's appeal was heard before Mr Justice Humphreys, who described the letter as the strongest link in the chain of evidence which had satisfied the jury of Heys's guilt. Dismissing the appeal, Mr Justice Humphreys commented: 'The writer of this letter is the person who killed that girl – he says so!' Arthur Heys was hanged at Norwich Jail at 9.0 in the morning of Tuesday 13 March 1945.

Twelve years later there was a postscript to this case which, although it had nothing to do with the murder, might be thought to give further credence to the belief that certain families are 'fated' to tragedy. Winnie Evans, the victim of the murder, was the fourth member of her family to die within a few years. In June 1957 a second member of the Heys's family also died a violent death. He was Arthur Heys's elder brother, Albert, then aged fifty, who was killed when he dived sixty feet from a steel tower into a tiny tank of water at a village fête at Halstead, Essex. He had been watching an acrobat perform this feat and shouted to the crowd: 'That's easy. I could do that.' Before anyone could stop him he rushed up the tower and made the dive – hitting the side of the tank and dying shortly after he had been dragged out by ambulance men.

If a young soldier had not torn his thumb on some barbed wire, and if the laboratory detectives had been less careful in their analysis of a strip bandage used to bind the wound, the murderer of Mary Angela Hagan might never have been brought to justice.

Mary, fifteen years old, was a well-built girl, five feet four inches tall, dark-haired and with eyes so sparkling that she was often called 'Merry Mary' by neighbours and friends in the Waterloo district of Liverpool, where she lived with her parents and younger brother John in Brookside Avenue. She was a bright girl, too, having won a scholarship to Seafield Convent, a secondary school, from the elementary school at which she started her education.

At 6.45 pm on Saturday 2 November 1940, Mary left her home to buy an evening newspaper and some cigarette papers for her father. She was known to have called at three shops, the shopkeepers remembering the pretty girl in her fur-trimmed brown coat, brown shoes and white knitted gloves. For some reason she cannot explain, Mary's mother began to feel anxious within twenty minutes of her daughter's departure. It was not unusual for the girl to be gone for an hour on an errand – she was so friendly and knew so many people in the neighbourhood that she often stopped to chat – but on this occasion Mrs Hagan was worried. 'I felt instinctively – I suppose it was a mother's intuition – that something dreadful had happened to her,' said Mrs Hagan. 'When neighbours realized how anxious I was they went to look for her. A search party was organized within less than an hour after Mary had left the house.'

In wartime blackout conditions, with no street lights and not a glimmer showing from the houses, this was not an easy task. It was extra difficult for Mary's father, shipping-clerk James Hagan, who had an artificial leg which made progress in the pitch darkness a slow and hazardous business. Mrs Hagan went with him, leaving eleven-year-old John in the house in case his sister returned while their parents were out. It was 11.30 pm before she was found, in a cement blockhouse (designed for occupation by the Home Guard) on a railway bridge only about a hundred yards from her home. She had been raped and strangled and there were bruises on her neck, which also bore one smudged thumbprint in dried blood. The cigarette papers were in a pocket of her coat and the evening newspaper she had bought was beside her.

It was raining hard that night and Mary's shoes were wet and muddy, but there was no sign of the girl having been dragged into the blockhouse. She had evidently been lured in, on some pretext, or carried in forcibly by her killer – which, even in densely populated Liverpool, could easily have happened without anyone seeing, in the total blackness of a moonless night and at a time when most people were hurrying to the shelter of their own homes.

Dr J. B. Firth, then Director of the North Western Forensic Laboratory, took samples of soil from the floor of the blockhouse and also retained for examination a little piece of material found near the body. This was so wet and muddy that it was at first impossible to identify it, but after cleaning, it was revealed as a bandage consisting of three layers of material, the outer one brown and the two inner layers impregnated with ointment. Analysis showed that the ointment contained acriflavine, a substance which was not in general use but was widely used in Civil Defence and Service dressings.

In peace time such a discovery would have narrowed the

field of inquiry considerably, but in 1940, when the majority of males were in either the Armed Forces, the Civil Defence or the Home Guard, its value did not at first seem very great. The police had very little evidence to help them. There was a report that a middle-aged man with a slouching walk had been seen hanging about near the blockhouse on several occasions. Descriptions were also issued of two soldiers seen in the vicinity. One of them was said to have had a badly scratched face and a bleeding thumb. He had stopped a woman and asked if he could clean himself up at her house because he had been involved in an accident.

Then on 13 November, eleven days after the murder of Mary Hagan, police picked up a soldier at Streatham, London, who was wanted for questioning in connection with an attack on a girl at Seaforth – a ten-minute train journey from Liverpool's Exchange Station.

This girl, Anne McVittie, a nineteen-year-old typist of Ford, Lancashire, told the police that on 4 October 1940 a soldier had pushed her from her bicycle as she was cycling home. When she tried to get up he had knocked her into a bank of stinging nettles. 'I screamed and he caught me by the throat,' she said. 'He punched and kicked me and told me he'd kill me if I didn't shut up. I persuaded him to release me and then, to gain time, I agreed to go into a field with him. But I ran away, dived into a canal and swam to the other side.' She added that she then saw the soldier ride away on her bicycle, taking her handbag with him. After he had gone she swam back across the canal, then walked home, eventually arriving in a state of complete exhaustion.

At a subsequent identity parade she picked out as her assailant the soldier the police had found in London – twenty-eight-year-old Irish Guardsman Samuel Morgan, of Berkeley Drive, Seaforth. When charged with assaulting Miss McVittie and stealing her cycle and bag containing £1 17s 6d, Morgan replied: 'I don't know anything about it.'

While he was in custody, awaiting trial on this charge, detectives noticed that on his right thumb Morgan had a wound which was beginning to heal and appeared to have been sustained about two weeks before. They remembered the bloody thumb-print on Mary Hagan's neck – and went straight

189

to Morgan's home. There his sister told them that 'Sam' had cut his thumb on some barbed wire on 31 October, and to stop the bleeding she had bound it with one of his Army-issue field dressings. There was a small length over, which he had told her to keep.

This piece of bandage was sent to Dr Firth for comparison with the bandage found beside Mary Hagan's body. The warp and the weft of the two pieces were identical and an unusual feature of both was a double row of stitching holes on the selvedge. Inquiries at the factory producing this type of bandage revealed that it was unusual for there to be more than one row of holes on the selvedge. It was rather like a postage stamp – a double perforation made it a rarity.

If Dr Firth had had any doubt about the two lengths of field dressing being originally one complete piece, it was dispelled by Mr Ronald Crabtree, of Vernon and Company the manufacturers of the dressing. He told detectives that there were very many forms in which the selvedge could be made and it was unlikely that two manufacturers would have exactly the same formation. 'The double row of stitching down the selvedge of both samples means that the selvedge itself must have been just turned under in the fold at the side of the pad,' he reported. 'These pads are folded by hand and sewn by machine, the machine operator being left to judge the exact point at which the ends of the pad shall be sewn to the bandage. As a consequence the rows of stitches when opened out vary considerably and it is most unlikely for two pads to be sewn in exactly the same way, and it is even more unlikely that two pads would be found bearing double stitches down the selvedge.'

Microscopic examination of the two pieces revealed such a close similarity in the ends that it was almost a certainty that one had been roughly torn from the other. In spite of the ragged ends, the three rows of double stitching coincided exactly when the two samples were placed flat on a table together.

An analysis of the soil from the blockhouse floor showed the constituents, and the proportions, to be very much the same as the dirt extracted from Morgan's uniform.

Morgan pleaded not guilty when he appeared before Mr

Justice Stable at Liverpool Assizes in February 1941, but after a trial which lasted a week the jury were out for less than an hour before they found him guilty of the murder of Mary Hagan. On 25 March his appeal was dismissed and in April it was announced that the Attorney-General had refused an application for a fiat to take the appeal to the House of Lords. Samuel Morgan was hanged at Walton Jail, Liverpool, on 9 April 1941 – one of the very few people to be convicted of murder almost entirely on scientific evidence.

With the formidable John Horwell in charge of the police team and Bernard Spilsbury, pathologist extraordinary, in the laboratory, the killer of widow Annie Kempson in 1931 really didn't stand a chance. Yet he almost went free – and might well have escaped conviction had it not been for some tiny fragments of paper and one infinitesimal thread of cotton.

Horwell, at that time a Detective Chief Inspector at Scotland Yard, was called to Oxford on the evening of August Bank Holiday, 1931, to investigate the murder of Mrs Annie Louisa Kempson at her semi-detached house, The Boundary, St Clement's Street. She had been dead for two days when she was found, on Monday 3 August, lying on the dining-room floor. She had been hit on the head several times, probably by a hammer, before being killed by the severance of an artery in the neck.

Mrs Kempson, aged fifty-eight, was the widow of an Oxford tradesman, owned a certain amount of property and was known to keep quite a lot of money in the house. The motive for the murder was obviously robbery because the whole house had been turned upside-down, but the killer had failed to find a box full of pound notes and some gold and had taken only a small sum of money which had been left in an obvious place. There were no fingerprints, nothing to give the police a lead, only the rather negative clue that Mrs Kempson must have known the murderer because the house had not been forcibly entered.

A house-to-house interrogation, covering a radius of one mile from St Clement's Street, gave Horwell his first break. A woman named Mrs Andrews said that a man who had previously sold her a vacuum cleaner had called at her home on the afternoon of Friday 31 July. He told her some story about having been robbed of all his money and she lent him 4s 6d. Later he returned to the house and asked if she could accommodate him for the night because he had missed his last bus home. She agreed to do so. When he left her house on the morning of Saturday 1 August, she noticed that he was carrying a new hammer and chisel, which were loosely wrapped in brown paper. A check on nearby shops revealed that the man had spent four shillings of his borrowed money on the purchase of these tools. Horwell then remembered that among a large collection of letters, visiting cards and miscellaneous papers at Mrs Kempson's home there was a receipt showing the purchase of a vacuum cleaner – one of the same make as that sold to Mrs Andrews. It was a safe deduction, as the two women lived within ten minutes' walk of each other, that the same salesman had supplied both.

Mrs Andrews was able to give the salesman's name and police forces throughout the country were alerted to look out for him: Henry Daniel Seymour, aged fifty, medium height, slim build, well-spoken. Before long a report came from Aylesbury, Buckinghamshire, to say that a man of that name had spent the night of 30–1 July at a hotel in the town and had left without paying his bill. During the afternoon of Saturday 1 August – the day Mrs Kempson was murdered – he sneaked back into his room at the hotel without being seen, but was stopped before he could get away again. When he admitted that he had no money to pay what he owed, the proprietor confiscated the suitcase that Seymour had just packed with his personal belongings.

Horwell unpacked the case and found, among clothing and toilet articles, an obviously newly washed hammer from which the maker's label had been removed, evidently with some difficulty because there were scratches where it had been scraped from the handle. There seemed little else of interest until Horwell turned the case upside-down and banged it smartly. From the corners fell what at first appeared to be mouldy breadcrumbs but which were in fact fragments of rolled-up paper. When these were dropped into a tooth-glass filled with water they slowly unfolded, rather like the dehydrated Japanese paper flowers popular with children of that period. Horwell

192

extracted each minute fragment, dried them and then fitted them together in jigsaw fashion. When he had finished this delicate task he was rewarded with the complete label from the hammer!

The tool was sent to Spilsbury for examination and at first it looked as though this could not have been the weapon which had caused the head injuries. The head of the hammer was fractionally smaller than the indentations on the unfortunate woman's skull. But supposing the killer wanted to make sure that the weapon was kept clear of blood? He would wrap the head in cloth which could afterwards be destroyed. Microscopic examination bore out this theory. Caught between the head and the handle of the hammer was one small thread of a cotton and linen mixture. The pathologist then experimented with different thicknesses of this type of material, each time banging the hammer hard on to a board. It did not take him long to produce an indentation which matched exactly, in size and shape, those on Mrs Kempson's head.

Seymour was traced to Brighton, Sussex, where he was staying with another widow, a Mrs Harvey, occupying a bedroom immediately above his landlady's room on the floor below. He had bored two holes in the floor of his room so that he could spy on Mrs Harvey, presumably to see if she had any hidden cash. Although he denied everything except the purchase of the hammer and chisel (' I was hoping to get a job as a carpenter,' he said) there was little doubt of his guilt. At Oxford Assizes in October 1931 he was convicted of the murder of Annie Louisa Kempson, and was hanged at Oxford Jail two months later.

Seymour had been a criminal for most of his adult life and, like many educated crooks (he was the son of a doctor and had had a comfortable childhood), he devised a number of grandiose schemes for making money. A plan for stealing jewellery from the British Museum fell through because, although in some remarkable way he had succeeded in getting facsimile keys of the jewel cases, his confederates lost their faith in him at the last moment and refused to carry through the operation. There was a similar eleventh-hour cancellation of his plan to acquire valuable jade from the burial-ground of rich Chinamen.

Undeterred by these failures, he made his money from rather more commonplace crimes like housebreaking and fraud and had been in and out of prison since the age of twenty. His job as a vacuum-cleaner salesman was not so much a way of earning a regular income as of getting to know suitable victims for robbery. The main reason for his desperate attempt to raise money at the time he killed Mrs Kempson was discovered by the police after his arrest. In the summer of the previous year he had assaulted a woman in Paignton, Devonshire during the course of a vacuum-cleaner demonstration – but had been placed on probation and ordered to pay her £10 compensation. He had not paid, though he had kept promising to do so. His period of one year's probation, and the final date for payment of the £10, expired on 1 August 1931. That was the day he murdered Annie Kempson.

11

Guilty or not guilty?

Scientific evidence played a dual part in a Manchester murder investigation that took place soon after the Second World War. It helped to prove – though not to the ultimate satisfaction of a number of people – the guilt of a man who denied all knowledge of the killing, and conversely, the innocence of a man who actually confessed to the crime.

The sordid story began to unfold when two children on their way home from Mass at a Roman Catholic Church on Sunday 20 October 1946 found the body of a woman on a bomb-site in Cumberland Street, near Deansgate, Manchester. She had been savagely battered about the head and a few feet away from the body was the weapon used in the attack, a rather unusual cobbler's hammer.

The victim was a prostitute, Olive Balchin (or Balshaw), also known as Lily Wise, but beyond that fact very little was discovered about her. The doctor who made the post-mortem examination described her as a woman of between forty and fifty years of age, with yellow hair turning grey, a few septic teeth in the lower jaw, and no upper teeth at all. If she had any relatives they were not prepared to come forward and she was eventually identified by a retired coal-wharf manager who had known her for about nine years but had not seen her for some time. He thought she came from Birmingham and believed her age to be thirty-eight to forty. She seemed to have no home, but had lived in a lodging-house in Manchester for a few weeks before her death.

On the day following the discovery of her body, a picture of the hammer was published in the daily newspapers, and there was a quick response from Mr Edward Macdonald, a second-hand dealer with a shop at 3 Downing Street, Ardwick, Manchester. He declared that it was one he had sold on the previous Saturday afternoon. Mr Macdonald was positive that it was the same hammer because, he said, he had bought it only a few hours before and had looked at it carefully. It was a type used by cobblers or leather-dressers and had an unusual shaft. He told detectives that a man had come into his shop between 5.0 and 6.0 pm on the Saturday and asked the price of the hammer. Mr Macdonald told him that it would cost 3s 6d and had pointed out that it would be no good for general purposes, such as knocking in nails. The customer had replied: 'It will suit my purpose.' Macdonald wrapped it in a piece of brown crêpe-paper and the customer left the shop with it in his raincoat pocket. The police showed the shopkeeper a piece of brown paper found near the body, and Macdonald maintained that it was identical with the piece that he had used to wrap the hammer when he sold it. He described the man who bought it as of medium build with a pale face and said the customer had been wearing a white shirt, dark tie, dark suit and a fawn raincoat.

Further information was given to the police by Mrs Elizabent Copley, of Heald Road, Rusholme, Manchester, employed as a waitress at Queen's Café, Deansgate. She said that Olive Balchin had been in the café between 10.30 and 11.0 on the night of Saturday 19 October, accompanied by an older woman and a man. When the trio departed the man was carrying a thin parcel, about a foot in length, wrapped in brown paper which he had placed under the table near his chair while they were drinking tea. Later that night Olive Balchin was seen in the company of a man by Mr Norman Mercer, licensee of the 'Dog and Partridge', Deansgate, who was taking his dog for a walk at about midnight. He did not know Olive Balchin, but recognized her description in the papers. He later identified her at the mortuary as the woman he had seen on 19 October. She and her male companion were standing on the corner of Cumberland Street and seemed to be arguing.

There was no clue to the identity of the man mentioned by Mr Macdonald, Mrs Copley and Mr Mercer – and no concrete confirmation that each had seen the same man – but a week after the murder the police were told about a lodger at the Services Transit Dormitory who had been behaving in an

196

odd fashion, refusing to speak to fellow-lodgers and wandering about by himself at nights. When they went to the hostel to interview the strangely reserved man they identified him as Walter Graham Rowland, aged thirty-eight, who had been demobilized from the Royal Artillery in June 1946 – a man who already had a conviction for murder.

At nineteen years of age he had attempted to strangle sixteen-year-old Annie Schofield and had been sent to Borstal for three years. During his trial the girl had said she had forgiven him because she thought he was joking. When he was released she married him and they had one child, a girl. In 1934 Rowland strangled his daughter, Mavis, then aged two years, with a silk stocking. He was sentenced to death, but the jury recommended mercy and the sentence was commuted to life imprisonment. He was released after six years upon volunteering for the army in 1940.

Rowland was asleep in bed when the two police officers, one of whom he knew, called at the hostel and told him that Inspector Stainton wanted to see him at the police station. He sat up in bed and asked: 'You don't want me for murdering that woman, do you?' Later he said: 'I am admitting nothing because it's a fool's game to do that. I can account for where I was. I was at home in New Mills when she was murdered. I did not come back to Manchester that night.'

After further questioning he admitted that he had returned to Manchester that night, but did not go into Deansgate. His story was that he had had some supper, then stayed at Grafton House in Hyde Road, arriving after 1.0 am. Told that inquiries would be made at Grafton House, Rowland said he had not stayed there but had spent one night at 36 Hyde Road. He admitted knowing Olive Balchin, but said he called her 'Lil'. He produced a doctor's card which showed him to be suffering from venereal disease and he told the police: 'It was a blow to find I had VD. I wanted to know where I got it. If I had been sure it was her I'd have strangled her. If she gave it to me she deserved all she got.'

He still emphatically denied having killed her. When he saw photographs of the woman taken after death, he said: 'I have got an uncontrollable temper, but that's not evidence, is it? I am sure I would not do that. It's possible the hammer was got to do a job with. I was not going to do a job that night. The fact that I went home proves that.' In a signed statement, made later, Rowland said that he first met Olive Balchin seven or eight weeks previously and they had twice had sexual intercourse. He suspected that she had given him venereal disease, so on Friday 18 October, he went to a café with her to try to find out if she also had the disease. He did not see her on the following day or night. He went to his parents' home at New Mills during the evening of 19 October to collect clean clothes, and on leaving took a bus into Stockport, arriving at about 10.0 pm. He had a few drinks at the Wellington Hotel, then got a bus to Ardwick, where he had some supper in a chip shop, booking into 36 Hyde Road at about 12.30 am and staying one night. He added: 'I have given the black shoes I was wearing on the Friday to a man for the price of a packet of fags. The raincoat I was wearing on Friday I had borrowed and I've given it back to an American known to all the boys by the nickname of "Slim".'

Police enquiries showed that he had not spent the night of 19 October either at the Grafton Hotel or 36 Hyde Road. He was put up for identification and was picked out by Mr Macdonald as the man who had bought the hammer and by Mrs Copley and Mr Mercer as the man they had seen with Olive Balchin.

At the North Western Forensic Science Laboratory an examination was made of the woman's clothing, the hammer and the paper in which it had been wrapped, Rowland's clothing, and samples from the ground where the body was found. The blood on the hammer was of group A, the same as the dead woman's, and there was some of that group on the vertical edge of the inside of the heel of Rowland's left shoe. There were faint blood-smears on the paper round the clean clothes Rowland had collected from his mother, but it was not possible to identify the group, neither was there any group identification of spots on Rowland's handkerchief. There were no bloodstains on his clothing.

Two grey hairs found on Rowland's jacket matched hairs taken from Olive Balchin's head. The turn-ups of Rowland's trousers contained fragments of brick dust, cement, charcoal, clinker and withered leaves of rose-bay willow-herb – a mixture which matched up with samples taken from the ground on which the body had been lying.

Dr J. B. Firth, then Director of the North Western Laboratory, reported that, since the weapon used in the murder was a short hammer, it would not have been possible for the woman's assailant to deliver such a concentrated series of blows from a standing position. It would have been necessary for him to crouch or kneel in a position that would have caused his trousers to pick up material from the ground. This could have gone directly into the turn-ups or could have been brushed there by hand in the process of removing the 'debris' from the knees of the trousers. 'The material in the turn-ups of Rowland's trousers contained quite an appreciable quantity of material common to the scene,' reported Dr Firth, 'and a comparatively small amount of fluff usually associated with material in trouser turn-ups. I agree that other blitzed sites may contain similar materials, but to pick up such a comprehensive collection requires very close contact with the ground in the region where all the various materials are present.' Dr Firth added that he had visited the scene of the murder three times without acquiring in his own turn-ups any of the material he found in the turn-ups of Rowland's trousers.

Rowland was charged with the murder of Olive Balchin and appeared before Mr Justice Sellars at Manchester in December, 1946, when counsel for the prosecution made these five points which, in his submission, indicated Rowland's guilt: on the day of the murder he bought the weapon with which the woman was killed; he was seen with her at 10.30 to 11.0 pm and again at midnight; his accounts of his movements, relating to the address at which he had stayed on the night of 19 October, had been proved untrue; his answers to the police provided a motive for the crime – the suspicion that he had contracted venereal disease from the victim; scientific evidence linked him with the victim and with the site of the murder.

Rowland, in court, denied that he was the man who bought the hammer and said that he did not see Olive Balchin on 19 October. He was mistaken in saying he spent that night at 36 Hyde Road; it was in fact the following night, 20 October, that he spent at that address. On the night of 19 October he stayed at 81 Brunswick Street, arriving at about 11.15 pm, just as the proprietor was going to bed.

This story was supported by Mr Frank Beaumont, the proprietor of a boarding-house at 81 Brunswick Street, who said that Rowland was definitely in the house when he (Beaumont) locked up and went to bed at 11.40. He was closely cross-examined about an entry in his visitors' book which gave Rowland's date of arrival, and also his date of departure as 19 October. Beaumont said that the second entry was a mistake as the date of departure was 20 October. When it was suggested that perhaps Rowland had arrived after midnight on the Friday, which would have been in the early hours of 19 October, had spent the rest of that night there and left later the same day, Beaumont replied: 'Walter Graham Rowland definitely did arrive on the Saturday.'

Mrs Agnes Rowland told the court that her son appeared at her home at 7.30 on 19 October. He was not wearing a raincoat or overcoat and was not carrying a parcel. His blue suit was his 'demob' suit, the only one he had, and he was wearing a brown striped shirt. After he had washed, he changed into a pale-blue shirt. She always did his laundry for him and he had never possessed a white shirt. He left the house at 9.20.

On Monday 16 December 1946, after a two-hour retirement at the end of the five-day trial, the jury – who, of course, knew nothing of his previous convictions – found Rowland guilty of the murder of Olive Balchin. He was asked if he had anything to say as to why sentence of death should not be passed. 'Yes, I have, my Lord,' he replied. 'I have never been a religious man, but as I have sat in this court during these last few hours the teachings of my boyhood have come back to me, and I say in all sincerity before you and this court that when I stand in the Court of Courts before the Judge of Judges I shall be acquitted of this crime. Somewhere there is a person who knows that I stand here today an innocent man. The killing of this woman was a terrible crime, but there is a worse crime being committed now because someone with the knowledge of this murder is seeing me sentenced today for a crime which I did not commit. I have a firm belief that one day it will be proved in God's own time that I am totally innocent of this charge, and the day will come when this case will be quoted in the courts of this country to show what can happen to a man in a case of mistaken identity. I am going to face what lies before me with the fortitude and calm that only a clear conscience can give.'

Rowland's statement from the dock was by no means the end of the story because on 22 January 1947 – five days before Rowland's appeal was due to be heard – another man confessed to Olive Balchin's murder.

He was David John Ware, thirty-nine-year-old labourer who had been discharged from the army in 1943 with a diagnosis of 'manic depressive psychosis' and had been in mental homes several times. He had come to the notice of the police on Monday 21 October 1946 – two days after the murder at Manchester – when he went into a Sheffield police station and said that he had stolen some money from the Salvation Army Hostel at Stoke-on-Trent on the previous Friday. As the hunt for Olive Balchin's murderer was then at its height, Ware was asked if he had been in Manchester on 19 October, and he replied in the negative. He was dealt with in the normal way and, on his own admission of theft, was sent to Walton Prison, Liverpool. He was there when Rowland was sentenced to death and it was to the Governor of Walton that he sent his confession of murder.

He said that he left Stoke-on-Trent on Friday 18 October, with money he had stolen from the Salvation Army hostel, where he worked as booking-clerk. He went to Manchester and stayed the night. On the following afternoon, 19 October, he decided to buy a hammer for the purpose of committing robbery with violence. After buying the hammer he met Olive Balchin and they went to a cinema together and later had coffee in a café. 'I did not know whether to leave her or not,' continued Ware's statement, 'but after finding a dark place not far from Piccadilly I decided to spend a while with her. The spot where we stopped was a place or building that I took to be bombed in the war. We went inside the ruins and stood for a short while near the entrance. We were quite close to each other and being so near she took the opportunity of going through my pockets. I was aware of this but did not show her. I was ate up with hatred and felt immediately that I'd like to kill her. I realized I had the hammer. . . . I suggested moving further inside where we could not be seen. She agreed to this. She was on my left and with my right hand I got the hammer out of my pocket. While she was in front I struck her a violent blow on the head. She screamed and before her scream lasted any length of time I struck her again and this time she only mumbled.'

Ware went on to say that he caught a bus to Stockport and on the following Monday surrendered to the police for the theft of the money at Stoke-on-Trent. Later he added that he did this as a 'cover up' as he thought he would be safer from detection in the hands of the police or in prison than he would if he was wandering about.

While he was on remand, he said, he read about the finding of the body and that an arrest was expected, but then purposely avoided reading the papers because he did not want to hear anything more about the murder. He heard from a fellow-prisoner that Rowland, who was unknown to him, had been convicted of the crime 'This information worried me a great deal,' he said. 'I knew that only a short time would elapse before that man's execution. I thought a great deal about it.'

As soon as Rowland's solicitor, Mr George Hinchcliffe, heard about this confession, he requested that Ware's testimony be put before the Appeal Court. This was refused on the grounds that it would constitute a trial for Ware and a retrial for Rowland, which was not within the province of the Appeal Court.

Rowland's appeal was adjourned until 10 February 1947, and was then dismissed. Mr Hinchcliffe immediately put Ware's confession before the Home Secretary, who appointed Mr John Catterall Jolly KC to inquire into the confession and any other evidence that had come to light since the trial and to report whether there were any grounds for thinking there had been a miscarriage of justice in the conviction of Rowland.

On 25 February Mr Jolly reported that he was satisfied that there were no grounds for thinking that there had been any such miscarriage of justice. There was a number of reasons for this decision. The first came when Ware retracted his confession. 'I had nothing to do with the murder,' he told Mr Jolly. 'I made these statements out of swank more than anything, I had a feeling all along that I wouldn't get very far with them. I also thought I was putting myself in the position of a hero. I wanted to see myself in the headlines. In the past I wanted to be hung seeing that life was really not worth living.'

Mr Jolly commented: 'I have considered the written statement in the light of my investigations and all the circumstances of the case and of my observation of Ware's manner, demeanour and mentality. I am satisfied that when Ware told me that he did not commit the murder he was then speaking the truth.'

Mr Jolly also pointed out that Mr Macdonald, Mrs Copley and Mr Mercer – who had all identified Rowland as the man seen with Olive Balchin – failed to pick out Ware at an identification parade.

The scientific evidence, which had helped to convict Rowland, equally helped to clear Ware. Dr Firth said that he examined Ware's clothing at the end of January. There were no bloodstains on the trousers and the turn-ups contained only the usual type of fibre commonly found in turn-ups, giving no evidence that he was ever on the bomb-site on which Olive Balchin's body was found.

Walter Graham Rowland, the first man ever to occupy the condemned cell at Strangeways Jail, Manchester, on two separate occasions, was hanged on 27 February 1947. On the night before his execution he wrote to his parents, protesting his innocence to the last. 'You know I have told you the truth all along,' he wrote, 'and you have promised never to doubt, or cease from seeking the truth of my total innocence. The truth will come out in God's own time, so just go on with this firm belief in your hearts. . . . hold up your heads for I die innocently. I die for another's crime.'

Rowland did not write to his wife, Annie, nor did she write to him. By the time he reached the condemned cell she was his ex-wife, having been granted a divorce on grounds of cruelty – the cruelty being the killing of their baby daughter twelve years earlier. The case was heard while Rowland was awaiting trial for the death of Olive Balchin, the divorce court sitting *in camera* so that nothing would be made public which might prejudice the jury.

So Walter Rowland was executed, his ex-wife began a new life, and the public soon forgot the sorry saga of the Manchester prostitute and the two men involved in the story of her killing.

In 1951 the whole case was brought into the open again because David John Ware, who four years previously had confessed to the murder of Olive Balchin, was found guilty of the attempted murder of another woman, declared insane, and sent to Broadmoor.

In this case he tried to get into conversation with a respectable, middle-aged widow who was sitting reading on Durdham Downs, Bristol. She moved away and he followed – within seconds the unfortunate woman was beaten about the head and blood was pouring over her face. Three days after the attack Ware walked into Bath Police Station and gave himself up, telling detectives: 'I don't know what is the matter with me. I keep on getting an urge to hit women over the head.'

In a later statement he said: 'I got into one of those moods in which I felt I wanted to kill somebody. The feeling got worse, and I decided to buy a hammer and kill a woman with it. I can't stop myself. . . . I intended to smash her head in, but after the first blow the head of the hammer came off. I thought the first blow would knock her unconscious, but it did not and she set up an awful scream. That is why I ran away and did not finish her off.'

After Ware had been sent to Broadmoor the question of a possible miscarriage of justice relating to Walter Rowland was raised in the House of Commons by Mr Sydney Silverman, Labour member for Nelson and Colne. He asked for a new inquiry, 'bearing in mind the recent development' which showed that Ware had an insane obsession to do the very thing which he had confessed to doing in the Olive Balchin murder case. Sir David Maxwell Fyfe, Home Secretary, replied that there was nothing in the recent charge brought against Ware to require any further inquiry or action. There was no reason to doubt the findings of the first inquiry into the case.

In March the following year, Mr Silverman again pressed for an inquiry to see if there had not been 'a grave miscarriage of justice' in the Rowland case. Sir David Maxwell Fyfe again replied that he was satisfied there had been no such miscarriage of justice.

'There is nevertheless a large body of opinion which is not without experience in this matter which considers that there is an established case here of the execution of a perfectly innocent man,' said Mr Silverman.

In a written reply, Sir David told Mr Silverman that he did not accept the suggestion that innocent men were hanged in this country and he knew of no foundation for any doubts alleged to exist.

There was a final postscript to the case in 1954 when, on 1 April, David Ware hanged himself from a window shutter in Broadmoor.